Angela, you are very special to the Lord. Wonderful things are in store for you. Ps. 37

Top Secrets REVEALED

Master Plan for the End Game

Third Edition, Expanded

Robert Mawire

Good News Publications
Dallas/Fort Worth

D1361969

Unless otherwise noted, all scripture references in this book have been obtained from **The King James Version**.

Third Edition, Expanded.
Original Title: <u>Exalted</u> <u>in</u> <u>Christ</u>: <u>A</u> <u>Spiritual</u> <u>Blast-Off</u> <u>to</u> <u>a</u> <u>New</u> <u>Dimension</u>.

Top Secrets Revealed: The Master Plan For The End Game
ISBN 0-9671185-0-6

Copyright ©1995, 1996, 1999 Robert Mawire.
Printed by : Book Crafters, 613 E. Industrial Drive, Chelsea, Michigan 48118-0370

Published by: Good News Publications,
P O Box 895, Ft. Worth, Texas, 76101.
Phone Orders: (800)853-7101
Fax: (817)801-3334
E-mail: hope@goodnewsworld.org

Contents

i

Be the Best!
Receive the Best!

Acknowledgments

I want to thank all those around the world who have encouraged me to share the top secrets of the master plan for the endgame. These eternal truths can lift you from aimless desperation to new heights.

The secrets in this book will transform you to be a success in life. They will radicalize you. They will open to you divine resources that are unparalleled and infinite. These are the keys that unlock the treasure house.

This book is a tribute to the Master Planner of my life, who showed me the secrets of a new dimension of living. The supernatural is available to all who dare to believe. Miracles still happen today.

Life is exciting for those walking at the center of God's master plan. My parents knew His plan and shared it with me. Now about ninety years of age, they are still full of vision and vitality. It's never too late.

I deeply appreciate the following people who helped to make this work a reality: Anne Rose, Jeannine and David Kuhnell, Dianne Diserens, Bill and Mary Hughes, Mashike Yoyo, Rick Kumpf, Chad Ide, and Al Hill III.

Finally, thanks to my precious (fair dinkum Aussie) wife, Janet, and my sons Jonathan, Caleb, and Stephen, who encouraged me to reveal the top secrets of the master plan for every one who dares to find out. Janet endured long hours typing the manuscripts, for which I am grateful.

To you, my reader—expect the impossible. God is bigger than all your problems.

Introduction

Discover the master plan. With the millennium fast approaching, the master plan for our destinies lies coded deep in the canons of the ancient scriptures. These secrets reveal pathways to life success, though this world seems bent on moral decline and economic collapse.

America's hour of crisis is ahead. However, God's word holds the keys to change life's difficulties into opportunities and its problems into prospects for success. It contains strategies to accelerate and actuate your future, which is hidden in God's master plan for the endgame.

Do you feel you're never going to get what you want in life? Are you afraid to take a risk? Are you tormented by a struggle in your soul, and held back by an ingrained negative attitude? It's not fun! It's not exciting! It's a humdrum, topsy-turvy, gloom-and-doom rat race to much nothingness.

Without a doubt, predictions of a global economic catastrophe and a millennium-bug aftermath are intensifying your fear of the future. Your attitude determines your altitude. Eagles ride the storm. They take advantage of turbulence to rise to new heights of glory. Eagle Christians choose Christ rather than crisis.

The Master Plan is risk free; its secrets have been proven again and again over a period of 6,000 years of recorded history. These kingdom secrets will impel you to a new dimension of successful living in the age of chaos. The only risk you take is by ignoring its pathway to unlimited success. Deep within your spirit is a divine potentiality ready to explode: Christ in you the hope of glory.

This book is not about the free-market system, though its secrets create an atmosphere of excitement, creativity, and innovation. It is about freeing your entrapped soul from the debilitating effects of your past, into the glorious liberty of the sons of God.

There is a master plan to your life. Find out what it is. Build your life according to the blueprint for abundant success and happiness that Jesus came to give you. Accept His plan! Embrace His promise: "I am come that they might have life, and that they might have it more abundantly." [1]

Seize the opportunity now, appropriate your abundant success. Your security in life is guaranteed by divine sovereignty because "Unto you it is given to know the mysteries of the kingdom of God"[2] ... the master plan.

Chapter 1

The Master Plan

There is a master design to the planetary order, a divine destiny for creation. Interwoven in it is an irreplaceable plan for your own success in life. The secrets of this master plan hold magnificent possibilities, guaranteed by divine sovereignty.

This divine potentiality is like the ocean waves, which God creates every day by sending the winds. Embracing these divine currents—as accomplished surfers do—will set a day-by-day pace in your life for excellence and the exhilaration of success.

This book puts at your disposal age-old, proven ways for you to ride the next wave to the pinnacle of divine power. You are the focal point of the master plan. You are at the center stage of the endgame. This is your hour. *Disappointment* is missing your appointment with the Master Planner of your life, the Lord Jesus—the Author and Finisher of your faith.[1]

You are created to pioneer new paradigms, pursue progressive revelation, and grasp your glorious destiny. Through God's grace, you *can* re-order your priorities, catch the wave, and ignite your soul with a vision of new beginnings. Let the glow of optimism and faith rise within you. There are limitless possibilities before you in Christ!

God wants to change the state of affairs that entangles you. Hope in God! Stop trying and start trusting. He has the master

1

plan for your life, and He wants to reveal to you these top secrets of the kingdom. Your endgame has begun. Your end is going to be greater than anything you ever imagined possible! Listen to what God says about it:

> Eye hath not seen, nor ear heard, neither have entered into the heart of man, the things which God hath prepared for them that love him.[2]

This is his personal promise to you. You can count on it. Wow, it's big! It's exciting! Best of all it's risk free, because it's guaranteed by God Himself. This is His master plan for your endgame. It was ordained before the foundation of the world simply because "You are his workmanship, created in Christ Jesus unto good works, which God hath before ordained that you should walk in them."[3]

This is not merely a concept to read about in the pages of scripture. This is real! The divine master plan for you is powerful and life-transforming. It is vital that you embrace it.

Many people's lives, for all practical purposes, exclude God's plan for them. For such people God is an occasional add-on convenience instead of the focus. God wants to be not the last-resort problem-solver, but the master planner and sustainer.

God's redemptive purpose in our lives is to restore us to a position of power and glory. God wants to set us free from wasting away in hopeless despair. Recognizing the master plan of His kingdom will give you insights that move you toward holiness. Holiness brings you happiness and intimacy with God.

These secrets are seeds that will cause you to grow on the inside into the image of your creator. They are not learned;

they are lived. They are not taught, they are caught. They activate your faith and ignite your soul! God has destined you to lead a life of success and accomplishment in every area of your life, without self-indulgence and self-glory.

The top secrets of the master plan for your life transform and translate you from the kingdom of darkness into the kingdom of God, a sphere of divine glory and majesty. In this heavenly involvement God promises to exalt you and to give you unlimited success in life:

> And it shall come to pass, if thou shalt hearken diligently unto the voice of the Lord thy God, to observe and to do all his commandments which I command thee this day, that the Lord thy God will set thee on high above all nations of the earth:
>
> And all these blessings shall come on thee, and overtake thee, if thou shalt hearken unto the voice of the Lord thy God.
>
> Blessed shalt thou be in the city, and blessed shalt thou be in the field. Blessed shall be the fruit of thy body, and the fruit of thy ground, and the fruit of thy cattle, the increase of thy kine, and the flocks of thy sheep. Blessed shall be thy basket and thy store. Blessed shalt thou be when thou comest in, and blessed shalt thou be when thou goest out.
>
> The Lord shall cause thine enemies that rise up against thee to be smitten before thy face: they shall come out against thee one way, and flee before thee seven ways. The Lord shall command the blessing upon thee in thy storehouses and in all that thou settest thine hand unto; and he shall bless thee in the land which the Lord thy God giveth thee.
>
> The Lord shall establish thee an holy people unto himself, as he hath sworn unto thee, if thou shalt keep

the commandments of the Lord thy God, and walk in his ways. And all people of the earth shall see that thou art called by the name of the Lord; and they shall be afraid of thee.[4]

When you move from the familiarity of religion to a relationship with God, when you push past threadbare images and pursue His master plan for your life, you will never be the same again. God will restore to you your glory. You were made for greatness. In Christ you are blessed with all spiritual riches, and in Him all of God's promises are *yea* and *amen*.[5]

Once you embrace God's master plan, the battle will be over and the endgame will begin. You are more than a conqueror in Christ Jesus, your Lord. God's magnificent grace has secured victory for you.[6]

The master plan is not merely to make you an obedient servant, but to manifest your sonship position of power and privilege. God's intention is that you may ultimately learn to reign with Christ and be conformed to his image, each day as you walk with Him. The Holy Spirit will empower you and lead you from glory to glory. He will execute the secrets of the master plan in your life.

This is not a religious book about the do's and don't's. It is about receiving the inheritance purchased for you by Christ on the cross. You can't earn what has been earned for you. The battle for your glorious future has been fought and won. The best is yet to come. Believe and receive!

God has made you free. Free from failure. Free from the do's and don't's. Free from the beggarly elements of the law. Free from the works of righteousness. Free from guilt and condemnation. Free from striving. Free in Christ to receive your sonship master plan for abundant joy and victory. Jesus is the end of the Law. Christ has been made unto you righteousness.[7] He is the end of the endgame.

This book is your survival handbook for rescue from a frustrating life of empty religiosity. You can now cross the gap between who you are, and who the Lord wants you to be. God's grace will give you access to the divine master plan for your life.

Your future does not depend upon your will power or skill power, but on divine power. Submission to God's will releases you from your ambition into His vision, and from your self-sufficiency into His sufficiency. God does not grant us what we deserve. He gives us what Christ purchased for us. In and of ourselves we do not measure up. He makes us complete in Him, by His grace alone.

In the eyes of the world, success in life results from your own determination and performance. But the world doesn't know the secrets of God. His plan for your life has predestined you for exaltation in Christ.

Jesus came to initiate God's plan of the ages for you. He is the author of the master plan. God wants us to tap into the secrets of the Kingdom mysteries, so we can appropriate all the riches of heaven as joint heirs. If you are sick and tired of dealing with lingering fears, doubts, wounds, and failures, you can give up and give in to Him Who will lead you from victory to victory. God is waiting for you to surrender to His master plan.

Chapter 2

Breakthrough

This book is about breakthrough! You need a breakthrough: a spiritual blast-off to new heights of glory and a new sphere of triumphant life. In the natural realm, the law of gravity holds you captive. But in the spiritual realm, Jesus has released you from the law of sin and death to the freedom of life in Him.[1]

The prophet Isaiah says, ". . . They that wait upon the Lord . . . shall mount up with wings as eagles."[2] God chose you before the foundation of this world[3] to be more than a conqueror in Christ Jesus.[4] The sovereignty of God guarantees you victory throughout time and eternity.

Jesus came from heaven to exchange your defeat for victory, your sorrow for happiness, your failure for success. He came to transform you into His own likeness.[5] He didn't come just to be an example of superabundant life. His purpose was to give you all that He had and all that He is, so that you too could experience heaven all the way to heaven.

In Christ Jesus, you are no longer earthbound. You are not limited to natural reality. You are seated with Him in the heavenlies.[6]

For too long, Christians have allowed ignorance to crush them under a load of despair and defeat. The Lord says in His word: "My people are destroyed for lack of knowledge."[7] Jesus demonstrated that true spirituality is not retreat from life but dominion, authority, power, and victory here and now.

Most people say Jesus' ultimate victory will take place only at the end of time. But every page in the Bible says we win every battle, and not just the war in the last chapter! We are overcomers through Him that loved us.[8]

The lukewarm church[9] conditions people to be good losers. Jesus came to liberate us from the paralyzing fear, doubt, and worthlessness that bind us from enjoying life to the fullest. He said, "I am come that they might have life, and that they might have it more abundantly."[10]

We have been chosen to receive abundant joy, abundant power, abundant peace, abundant prosperity. Believing Christians are destined for glory and dominion today. As David said, God is your glory and the lifter of your head.[11] In His presence there are fullness of joy and pleasures for evermore.[12]

Isaiah says, "No weapon that is formed against thee shall prosper, and every tongue that shall rise against thee in judgment thou shalt condemn. This is the heritage of the servants of the Lord."[13]

The apostle Paul triumphed over the negativity that opposed his ministry work, because he knew, "If God be for us, who can be against us?"[14] He told the Philippian church, ". . . My God shall supply *all* your need according to his riches in glory by Christ Jesus."[15]

7

This is a book about who you are in Christ. You have a new identity, a new nature, a new origin. You are born from above. ". . . Ye are a chosen generation, a royal priesthood, an holy nation, a peculiar people; that ye should show forth the praises of him who hath called you out of darkness into his marvellous light."[16]

God's election is eternal. Your position is fixed for time and eternity. "Faithful is He that calleth you, who also will do it."[17] It is not what you are doing for God; it is what He did and what He is doing in you and through you.

All that you have, all that you are is by His grace alone. The perseverance of the believer is nothing but the preservation of the Lord, because ". . . In me (that is, in my flesh,) dwelleth no good thing."[18]

Jesus best explained it when He said to His disciples. "For without me ye can do nothing."[19] The apostle Paul told the Ephesians that they were destined for fruitful lives in Christ: "For we are his workmanship, created in Christ Jesus unto good works, which God hath before ordained that we should walk in them."[20]

Through Jesus, God has made an unending covenant to bless us. He preordained us for greatness and glory in Christ Jesus before the foundation of this world.

The defeatist sermonettes of the lukewarm church are hindering God's Kingdom children from rising up. ". . . Greater is he that is in you, than he that is in the world"![21] God can be as great as we allow Him to be in and through us. The more we decrease, the more He increases.

I commit this book to God's people who have felt there is more. Yes, there is much, much more for you in Christ Jesus. The scripture says, "They . . . limited the Holy One of Israel."[22] Let go and let God have His way in you. If you believe, you will see the glory of God.

All things are possible to those who believe![23] Believe the word. Confess the word. Act the word. God promises to back His word: "For I will hasten my word to perform it."[24]

Chapter 3

The Master Plan for Transformation

Jesus came to earth and walked with man for one purpose: to bring us back to union and communion with God. The blood of Jesus reconciled us to God, and the Holy Spirit unites us in sweet fellowship with God. That daily intimacy and communion with God flows out of our relationship to Him as sons. As we abide in God, our union with Him can be seen in our daily walk by the fruit of the Spirit.

> Abide in me, and I in you. As the branch cannot bear fruit of itself, except it abide in the vine; no more can ye, except ye abide in me. I am the vine, ye are the branches: He that abideth in me, and I in him, the same bringeth forth much fruit: for without me ye can do nothing.[1]

The apostle Paul explains that this mystery of our union with Christ was accomplished in Christ's death and resurrection. When He died, we died. When He rose, we rose.

> I am crucified with Christ: nevertheless I live; yet not I, but Christ liveth in me: and the life which I now live in the flesh I live by the faith of the Son of God, who loved me, and gave himself for me.[2]

My old nature was crucified with Christ because the "old me" was at enmity with God. I wanted to be God and run my own life. The truth of the matter is the devil ran my life, because man is a vessel that contains either God or the devil.

Man is depraved. Ever since the fall of Adam, my old nature has been disposed to obey Satan rather than God. The law failed because of my flesh. But God put my old man in Jesus and crucified Him. It's no longer I that live, but Christ who lives in me.

The new me exists in union with Christ through the indwelling Spirit. When we receive Jesus, He makes us into new creatures who are one with Jesus in God. When God sees us, He sees Jesus in us.

God has made all things new in our lives, in order to make us capable of union life. The old nature of me-centeredness is gone. Jesus is now enthroned as Lord of my life. The destiny of the new humanity is to be everything that Jesus is and to possess all that God gave to Jesus Christ.

We are the branches, and Jesus is the vine. As branches we have no life of our own: we draw our life from the vine. The branches express the life of the vine through fruit-bearing. Through the branches or the body of Christ, the glory of God is seen on earth.

The Spirit empowers human channels to fulfill the will of God, as He determined before the foundation of the world.[3] The will of God is being done on earth as it is in heaven.[4]

However, our old nature bore fruit that reflected our depravity. The highest good that flesh could produce was, in God's sight, only like filthy rags, because nothing acceptable was living inside us.[5] Apart from Jesus we could do nothing. We produce "after our own kind."[6] Flesh produces flesh. The spiritually dead produces dead fruit.

Jesus said, "He that is not with me is against me."[7] That means that to be apart from Jesus is to be a servant of Satan. There is no neutrality in spirituality, no middle ground in the kingdom of God. The lukewarm He will spew out of His mouth.[8]

You cannot go halfway with Jesus, because to go with Jesus is to go all the way. Jesus does not want to be the first one in your life, but the only one. If He is not Lord of all, He doesn't want to be Lord at all. It's all or nothing with Him, just as it was at Calvary.

As for us, He is all we need! It's a deception to think that we need more than Jesus for our happiness. He is our sufficiency. We are complete in him.

Union: the Basis of Christ-likeness

We are Christ-like when Christ lives in us. Adam was Godlike when he walked together with God in the Garden of Eden. Jesus has redeemed us and restored us to our Father, so we can walk with Him again.

Our new man is one with Christ, justified, sanctified, and glorified in him. As we keep our new man in union with Christ, we grow to resemble Him: we reflect more and more His nature in our daily walk. This way of living is not a legalistic, disciplinarian, morbid will-religion of self-righteousness, but a happy, carefree, spontaneous celebration of life in Christ.

In the Christ-in-you union life, Christ does it all. You are simply a channel and not the source. Paul made clear Who is the origin: "For it is God which worketh in you both to will and to do of his good pleasure."[9]

God is constantly engaged in our lives to bring to pass His sovereign design, set in motion by the cross. He continues to apply the finished work of redemption in our lives. God's grace is vital not only for saving us, but also for making us holy and for bringing us to the glorious state for which He created man.

Our growth in Christ remains God's prerogative. He is the author and finisher of our faith. Our will power will not improve or add anything to the work of the Holy Spirit. Flesh has no legal part in what God is doing in us and through us.

Walking in Jesus' Footsteps

Looking at Jesus as our example only brings condemnation to the flesh, because we are never good enough. We never measure up. In the body of Christ, there is a great emphasis on walking in Jesus' footsteps. This is impossible. How can flesh walk in God's footsteps?

Flesh cannot cope with the holiness walk. It is easy to talk the talk, but impossible to walk the talk. Only through Christ in us can we walk the talk. He is in us to will and to do of His good pleasure. A branch cannot bear fruit apart from the vine. Without Jesus, we can do nothing.

The purposeful call of God upon your life cannot fail: "For whom he did foreknow, he also did predestinate to be conformed to the image of his Son."[10]

"God, who . . . calleth those things which be not as though they were,"[11] sees us as we can be, and He is able to bring about our growth into the image of Jesus. The sovereignty of God does not act against our will, but in harmony with our new nature.

In Christ Jesus, we have been newly created to do good works.[12] He has given us a new heart and a new spirit.[13] We can do all things through Christ who strengthens us.[14]

Justification by Faith Alone

In order for us to appreciate justification, we need to understand what it is. Justification is a divine act of grace, by which God puts us in right standing with Himself. This is a sovereign initiative of God; He chose to declare us free from sin. "It is God that justifieth. Who is he that condemneth?"[15]

Justification is a legal declaration, brought about by Christ's death and resurrection. We have been completely acquitted, "Being justified freely by his grace through the redemption that is in Christ Jesus."[16]

Therefore being justified by faith, we have peace with God through our Lord Jesus Christ: By whom also we have access by faith into this grace wherein we stand, and rejoice in hope of the glory of God. [17]

Justification is a judicial or forensic act. It is God's acquittal of us in Christ. Sanctification, on the other hand, is the practical outworking of our justification or our new legal status in Christ. Justification is our position in Christ, and sanctification is our possession in Christ.

True righteousness is wrought in us by God, after He declares us justified. This living quality of righteousness comes through faith. The works of righteousness cannot justify man. Human holiness is either suppression or denial of the flesh.

Most Christians live under constant stress, caused by this inner conflict between the law of God and their own depravity. Paul says, "For I know that in me (that is, in my flesh,) dwelleth no good thing: for to will is present with me; but how to perform that which is good I find not. For the good that I would I do not: but the evil which I would not, that I do."[18]

However, when we understand our new position in Christ Jesus, that revelation frees us from the power of sin.

Justification is an act of divine grace based on Jesus' fulfillment of the law, on our behalf. Jesus paid the full penalty for our sins. Therefore God's justification of the sinner is not a deviation from His holy law, but an acceptance of Jesus' atonement for sin. "For as by one man's disobedience many were made sinners, so by the obedience of one shall many be made righteous."[19]

Jesus' perfect obedience unto death makes right standing with God available to us, to realize and appropriate by faith.

Knowing that a man is not justified by the works of the law, but by the faith of Jesus Christ, even we have believed in Jesus Christ, that we might be justified by the faith of Christ, and not by the works of the law: for by the works of the law shall no flesh be justified.[20]

Chapter 4

The Blood of Jesus

We were purchased by the blood of Jesus. The blood of Jesus satisfies the divine demands of holiness. In Egypt, Israel put the blood of a lamb on the lintel and side posts of the door and secured immunity from the death angel.[1] Centuries before, the blood of a lamb was the foundation of the covenant relationship that entitled Israel to the blessings God gave Abraham. Even so, the blood of Jesus has brought us into covenant relationship with God.

All divine covenants are established by blood. The day we receive the blood of Jesus as the only basis of our righteousness and salvation, we are born again. We are freed from the slavery of sin. We enter into intimate relationship with God. We become a new creation in Christ.[2]

Calvary destroyed the power of Satan over us for all eternity. The price of our redemption was paid in full. The blood of Jesus reconciled us to God the Father.[3]

All mankind has now been put under the Abrahamic covenant. We are entitled to all of Abraham's blessings, because Jesus removed the curse of the law.[4] The cross proclaims our emancipation. In the new covenant, God has brought both Jew and Gentile together in Jesus. Jesus is now our new Passover Lamb.

We have passed over from death unto life, from slavery to sonship, from sorrow to happiness, from darkness to light. Our salvation, sanctification, and glorification are guaranteed by the blood of Jesus our Lord.

The New Covenant

The new covenant that Jesus made is a complete realization and a fulfillment of all the Old Testament covenants and messianic promises. The mystery hidden through the ages was that the new covenant would be with both Jew and Gentile.

Jeremiah foretold of the new covenant. Under the old covenant, man tried and failed to keep God's law. In this new agreement, however, God's grace inscribed it on the heart.

But this shall be the covenant that I will make with the house of Israel; After those days, saith the Lord, I will put my law in their inward parts, and write it in their hearts; and will be their God, and they shall be my people.[5]

The covenant the Spirit showed Jeremiah was established by Jesus through His death and resurrection. This new covenant is superior to all other covenantal systems in its power to transform people from within their hearts. In previous dispensations, the law was the external, holy demand of God.

In addition to a renewed heart, the sinner who accepts God's offer of the new covenant receives justification and salvation, together with adoption into Gods family. This covenant relationship is one-sided. God does everything. He forgives iniquity and remembers it no more. He writes the law into the heart. He declares himself responsible for those yielded to Him. God takes total initiative, and man is only a receiver of the divine grace.

The new covenant brought forth the full fruition of all God's redemptive purposes. Understood in its total Biblical setting, this covenant is with "whosoever will," both Jew and Gentile. This does not oppose His promises to His chosen people, for it secures the perpetuity, future conversion, and blessing of Israel. The Jewish people will be included in the numberless multitudes from every tribe, language, and nation at the end of the time of the Gentile.

In this new covenant, the individual believer can go into the holy of holies[6] and have intimate fellowship with God the Father in Jesus' name. Jesus is our High Priest,[7] mediating between us and God, not on the basis of lamb's blood but of His own sacrifice.

Jesus shed His blood for the remission of our sins.[8] He opened for us a new and living way into the holy of holies, and made us acceptable to God by giving us His holiness. He sealed our eternal salvation by granting us the Holy Spirit, as an earnest[9]—a down payment—of that which is to come. Our eternal security as believers is in the fact that He promised never to leave us or to forsake us.[10]

Confession of Possession

The human mind, until it is renewed by the word, is not conscious of divine acquittal, justification, and sanctification, because reason cannot attain to spiritual truth. It is hidden to the carnal mind. The believer can know in only one way: by the revelation of the word. The word reveals the unfathomable riches we have in Christ.

The word was written by the Spirit and can be interpreted only by the Spirit. Only then does the written word become the living word. The Holy Spirit is the executor of the covenant or will. Salvation, justification, and sanctification become real in our lives by our confession of faith in the revealed word.

God's written testimony about Himself and us is final. It is God's eternal declaration that cannot be changed. When we confess what God has said, He backs it up. Jesus overcame the devil by "It is written."[11] We defeat hell by "It is written." When we stand on "It is written," the devil flees.

It is written: Greater is He that is in you than he that is in the world.[12] It is written: Jesus has been made righteousness unto us.[13] It is written: As He is, so are we.[14]

"It is written" settles once and for all every question the mind may bring up. The only thing to doubt is our doubts. Feelings lie, appearances lie, common sense lies. Only "It is written" is true. Jesus said, ". . . The truth shall make you free."[15] "It is written" renews our minds and frees our emotions from fear and guilt. God has said the last word: "Be of good cheer; I have overcome the world."[16]

The confession of our faith always possesses the promises of God. What we believe in our hearts, we must declare with our lips, because confession is possession. Salvation, justification, and sanctification are divine acts of grace to be made our own by affirming them as fact. The faithfulness of God guarantees the manifestation.

Thinking Like God

The word of God is God thinking aloud. We appropriate God's thoughts by reading God's word. Our will becomes conformed to God's will, as we walk in the truth and meditate on the word. However, the carnal mind is controlled by appearances and externals. Therefore it is unstable, tossed to and fro like waves of the sea.[17]

Right thinking leads to right action. When you think the word, you will do the word. Jesus wants us to be doers of the word.[18] The word renews the mind and changes our emotional state, so that the Holy Spirit can shape our deeds to conform to God's will.

Christians must be established in the word, because outlook determines outcome. Word-based outlook produces divine outcome or blessings. "For as he thinketh, so is he."[19]

We must think the word, so we can be what God wants us to be. Every promise in His word directly reveals what God is eager to do for us. We must act decisively on the basis of the word, against all opposing

21

elements and mountains of difficulties that may seem to block our way. Our faith turns pressure into praise, and confesses victory before the results come in, because He that promised is faithful.[20] He will not fail.

The word must become flesh in our lives.[21] Faith without action is dead.[22]

Chapter 5

Faith: Title Deed to the Supernatural

The modern man has exalted reason above revelation. Reason and emotional feelings belong to the natural man. He is controlled by externals, but faith in the word belongs to the supernatural man, who trusts invisible evidence. The carnal man believes that only natural evidence is conclusive, denying the eternal evidences of the written word.

The word is eternal substance. It is a title deed to the divine property that Jesus purchased for us. "Now faith is the substance of things hoped for, the evidence of things not seen."[1]

Faith is the certificate of deposit of the unseen things. It is a documented letter of credit, issued by the Bank of Heaven, to be honored on sight. Faith draws out the unseen things by its confession and praise. The word of God is bankable! God honors it on sight. All claims are to be made in Jesus name.

The Constitution of God's Kingdom

The Bible is heaven's constitution, overriding or overturning all carnal decisions as unconstitutional. In the Kingdom of God, the Bible is the supreme law of the land and therefore final. It settles all matters. The word completely annuls all contrary evidence.

Christians live in a sphere of divine sovereignty. This is what it means to say Jesus is Lord. God backs His word with all His power and might as the supreme Ruler of the universe. He is the Alpha and Omega.[2]

Faith confesses the impossible done in Jesus' name, because Jesus said, "All things are possible to him that believeth."[3] Real faith lays hold of the promises of God until they are fulfilled; therefore, confession brings possession.

Faith is the language of victory. The Holy Spirit empowers us to overcome Satan's illegal occupation of the redeemed or purchased property. God will defend His word. The confession of faith makes it a fact.

Accepting the Will as Final

The death of Jesus, the testator, makes His will effective, entitling us to every blessing in heaven. Faith dares to stand in the face of circumstantial evidence and declares, "God will do what He said He will do." Faith declares while the battle is raging, "We are more than conquerors through him that loved us."[4]

The will exposes the enemy as a con artist and a defeated foe. Despite the enemy's relentless attack, the will proclaims that all power has been given to Jesus. He has passed on to every believer the authority to use that power. The devil tries to steal what Jesus purchased for us in His death and resurrection, but God says, ". . . Resist

the devil, and he will flee from you."[5] Do not allow him
to steal your initiative.

The Source of Doubt: Knowledge of Good and Evil

From the fall, man's common sense has been wrong.
The Bible is the only source of truth. To believe the word
is to believe the truth.   The fact that the scripture
disagrees with our five senses proves that the depraved
natural man cannot arrive at the divine will by reason. ".
. . The carnal mind is enmity against God: for it is not
subject to the law of God, neither indeed can be." [6]

Common sense is natural and is not subject to the
word. Though reason may make a lot of sense, the word
of God must always overrule it. The word is greater than
reason, because God is greater than man. The word is
greater than reality.   God stands behind His word to
perform it.[7]

The word is eternal, but reality is temporary. The
supernatural is greater than the natural, the divine greater
than the human. The invisible is greater than the visible.

Through faith we understand that the worlds were
framed by the word of God, so that things which
are seen were not made of things which do appear.
[8]

The Prayer of Faith

The effectual fervent prayer of a righteous man
availeth much.[9]

The prayer of faith is based upon absolute certainty of the will of God. When you are wondering whether something is God's will or not, you cannot pray a prayer of faith. The prayer of faith is not based upon hope, but on divine guarantees in the word. The prayer of faith is asking God to fulfill His promise.

When you know God's promise, you are on firm ground. Prayer based upon wishful thinking is unsteady and uncertain of God's will. James tells us that such a wishy-washy prayer is not answered.

> But let him ask in faith, nothing wavering. For he that wavereth is like a wave of the sea driven with the wind and tossed. For let not that man think that he shall receive any thing of the Lord.[10]

Ignorance of the clear will of God makes it hard to be steadfast. In such cases we need the word of God to reveal God's will, before we can pray with confidence. Faith is built upon the solid foundation of God's eternal and unchangeable word. The prayer of faith is certain, because it is grounded on the word—the revealed will of God.

> And this is the confidence that we have in him, that, if we ask anything according to his will, He heareth us: And if we know that He hear us, whatsoever we ask, we know that we have the petitions that we desired of him.[11]

It is certainly a great joy to know that the prayer we have offered has been heard, and that what we have asked for has been granted, before we receive the manifestation.

The word gives us certainty to go ahead and to thank God for the answer, immediately after the prayer. We have the confidence to praise God for the answer, without visible natural evidence.

Our confidence is based upon God's faithfulness. We have faith that God will do what He said in His word, because He has never failed, in 6,000 years of human history.

Blessed be the Lord, that hath given rest unto his people Israel, according to all that he promised: there hath not failed one word of all his good promise, which he promised by the hand of Moses his servant.[12]

God is not a man, that he should lie; neither the son of man, that he should repent: hath he said, and shall he not do it? or hath he spoken, and shall he not make it good? [13]

Our confidence is not based on vain speculation. God has a proven track record. He backs His word with all His power and might. His sovereign will is going to be done, on earth as it is in heaven. "For I will hasten my word to perform it."[14] History bears record that He never failed His children.

The Father's heart is to bless His children, and His promises express His will. He wants to meet all our needs above and beyond all that we can ask or think.[15] His thoughts toward us are of peace.[16] He came that we might have abundant life.[17] God wants us to have the best.

No critic can point to one word or promise that God gave that He failed to fulfill. He is Lord of history. He is the Alpha and the Omega. He is the first and the last.[18] All things were created for His pleasure.[19] All flesh is like a drop in a bucket.[20] He is the Lord of lords, and the King of kings.[21]

Unlocking the Power That Created the Universe

The power of the word created all things, and you cannot separate God from His word. Unbelief in the word is unbelief in God. The body of Christ needs to cast aside all its reasonings and head-knowledge and rely on the word of the God who calls those things that are not as if they were.[22]

The tragedy of the modern Church is its confidence in human intellectual capacity and its lack of dependence on God's power. The Church's harvest should not be surprising, "For he that soweth to his flesh shall of the flesh reap corruption; but he that soweth to the Spirit shall of the Spirit reap life everlasting."[23]

God has revealed His will in his word, because He can actualize His will only as our prayers harmonize with it. The prayer of faith is agreeing with God's declared will for our lives. It is a human response to God's initiative. ". . . Not my will, but thine, be done."[24]

Therefore prayer is man's willing alignment with the sovereign will of God: "If we ask anything *according to his will*, he heareth us: And if we know that he hear us, whatsoever we ask, we know that *we have the petitions* that we desired of him"[25]

28

When we base our prayer on a definite promise in the word, we know we are praying in agreement with God's will, because God will never act against His word. It is in such times *that we know we have the petition that we ask of Him.* This is when faith is persistent, because it sees the end from the beginning. Faith sees Satan defeated even when he is like a roaring lion, seeking whom he may devour.[26]

The shout of victory precedes victory. By faith, we see the wall come tumbling down. We see Goliath dead. We run like David to the battle ground. The prayer of faith releases the eternal power of God, inherent within the word to accomplish its desired purpose in time.

The carnal man, who is controlled by the five senses, cannot rise above visible reality. That is why our old man must be crucified with Christ, so that our "new man" in Christ, who walks not by sight but by faith,[27] could come forth. By faith we reckon ourselves dead to the sin of this world and alive unto God,[28] and thus we are able to do all things through Christ who strengthens us.[29]

Finding the Will of God

The question most Christians have is how to pray for a space-age issue for which there is no clear scripture. First, the word tells us there is nothing new under the sun.[30] The word addresses the whole man in the whole world, for all ages. However, there are some personal matters where we don't have a definite promise in the word to base our faith on. In such situations, can we know God's will? Yes, in many cases we can. Paul answers that question in his letter to the Romans.

Likewise the Spirit also helpeth our infirmities: for we know not what we should pray for as we ought: but the Spirit itself maketh intercession for us with groanings which cannot be uttered. And he that searcheth the hearts knoweth what is the mind of the Spirit, because he maketh intercession for the saints *according to the will of God.*[31]

Jesus said He would send His disciples a Comforter[32]— *paraclete* in Greek, meaning counselor, helper, or advocate. The Holy Spirit is given to comfort us and to carry all our cares to the Father by interceding for us.[33] First, the Spirit of God knows the sovereign will of God for our lives in every circumstance we face each day. Second, the Holy Spirit aligns our own wills to God's will as we abide in Him. The paraclete is in us to will and to do of the Father's good pleasure.

Jesus said it was to the disciples' advantage that He was going away.[34] The Lord's glorification made possible for us a deeper and a more constant daily intimacy with God in the Spirit. When we abide in Him, and He abides in us,[35] we are not uneasy about knowing His will, because to God relationship comes before performance.

Our mission is to know Him, because our call is to sonship and not to servanthood. We are anxious about nothing, when God is in control of everything in our lives. Like Israel, we are carried on wings of the Spirit: "Ye have seen what I did unto the Egyptians, and how I bare you on eagles' wings, and brought you unto myself." [36]

Common sense would have been to take the Egyptian highway to Canaan. Everybody knew the way, but God doesn't use the common-sense way to lead His children. His ways are higher than our ways. His thoughts are higher than our thoughts.[37]

God's way dead-ends at the Red Sea, with the Egyptians behind them. He outsmarted the enemy. God led Israel through the Red Sea and the wilderness in a truly unique and marvelous way, never to be repeated. God didn't give them a road map. He gave them Himself.

Absolute surrender leads to absolute victory. We do not need to know the way, because He is the way.[38] We do not need to know how, because He carries us on eagles' wings.

All guidance proceeds from intimacy with the Father. We are not led by biblical principles or Judeo-Christian ethics, but by the Spirit. "The just shall live by faith."[39]

Jesus sent the Paraclete to *hodegeo*, which means in Greek to "guide." The Comforter is the guide. The Holy Spirit who abides in us will lead us from victory to victory, and from glory to glory. He will pray us through to divine will. We need to learn to be still, so we can hear His still, small voice saying, "This is the way, walk ye in it."[40]

But the Comforter, which is the Holy Ghost, whom the Father will send in my name, he shall teach you all things, and bring all things to your remembrance, whatsoever I have said unto you.[41]

Chapter 6

Predestined for Glory

The Lord has entitled and ordained each member of his kingdom to share the same glory that He gave to Jesus. Our entitlement secures for us great and precious promises, which we can possess by faith. Knowing this produces in us absolute confidence. God has elected us to fulfill his eternal design of the ages in Christ Jesus.

Just as God manifested himself in the person of Jesus, we also express Christ's character to the world.

Whereby are given unto us exceeding great and precious promises: that by these ye might be partakers of the divine nature, having escaped the corruption that is in the world through lust.[1]

We must see ourselves in a new identity. The new creation is born to show forth His glory, throughout the ages to come: "That we should be to the praise of his glory, who first trusted in Christ."[2]

The Lord told Joshua about the land of milk and honey that was waiting to be conquered, "Every place that the sole of your foot shall tread upon, that have I given unto you, as I said to Moses."[3] Like Joshua, we must press through the veil of flesh-consciousness and sin-consciousness and into the liberty of the spirit. Joshua possessed the land by walking on it. We too walk the land with God.

We are well able to overcome the giants in our own lives, by fixing our eyes upon Jesus and not on the enemy. Through Him that loves us, we are more than conquerors, because—

> Even when we were dead in sins, [God] hath quickened us together with Christ, (by grace ye are saved;) And hath raised us up together, and made us sit together in heavenly places in Christ Jesus:[4]

Our union with Christ entitles us to all that Jesus is and to all of heaven's glory. But it is up to us to claim that heirship. Though Christ has secured our inheritance for us, it can be appropriated only by faith. We must determine to rise up violently against any power of hell or lust of the flesh that could keep us from obtaining what is rightfully ours in Christ.

> For we are his workmanship, created in Christ Jesus unto good works, which God hath before ordained that we should walk in them.[5]

We must look not at the bigness of the situation but on the bigness of our God. When we fully recognize that God is with us, our fears will melt away. We must see ourselves in Christ unshakable, unconquerable, and victorious, able to penetrate the enemy's walls of resistance.

All that God desires of us is that we receive the wonderful power of His restoring grace. It is a gift. We cannot earn what Jesus earned for us, nor can we achieve what He achieved for us. A believer is a receiver. God requires us to open ourselves to receive measureless grace, unlimited mercy, and abundant righteousness in Christ Jesus.

Recognizing our completeness in Christ is strength-imparting, mind-renewing, soul-cleansing, and heart-rejoicing. This is an undeniable and irrefutable truth. We must be certain deep within that the weapons of our warfare are mighty through God, to the pulling down of strongholds.[6]

Christ in us sanctifies, and Christ through us bears fruit. The fruit of the spirit is the proof of Christ's divine personality living in us. We have been grafted into Him, and His life flows in us.

I am the vine, ye are the branches: he that abideth in me, and I in him, the same bringeth forth much fruit: for without me ye can do nothing.[7]

We are channels of divine attributes and nature. The more we decrease, the more He increases in us. Our great potential in Christ comes forth to perfection in one way—through obedience.

We are not complete yet. We are His workmanship that He created *unto* good works. As we behold Jesus, God is making us into Jesus' image. In one sense, we can never fully reach the ultimate perfection unto His likeness, but the Holy Spirit is leading us from one degree of glory to another.[8] This is God's sovereign initiative. Our perfection is a work of His grace.

34

For whom he did foreknow, he also did predestinate to be conformed to the image of his Son, that he might be the firstborn among many brethren. Moreover whom he did predestinate, them he also called: and whom he called, them he also justified: and whom he justified, them he also glorified.[9]

We mature into Christlikeness by grace. Abiding in Him imparts this unattainable bliss to us. He is our perfection. He is our holiness. He is our joy. Because He abides in us, we can abide in Him.

In times of testing, we marshal strength and a sense of security from knowing we belong to Him and that we are in God. It is not who we are, but *whose* we are.

So that we may boldly say, The Lord is my helper, and I will not fear what man shall do unto me.[10]

This revelation is the blessed assurance that, no matter what, all things work together for them that love God.[11] We are more than conquerors through Him.[12] He is able to keep that which I commit to Him.[13]

God is the author and finisher.[14] From the moment we are born again, He begins to perfect us into His express image, and He continues throughout our lives. We are anointed and appointed unto good works that He ordained before the foundation of the world.

God will mold only a yielded vessel. The anointing breaks the bondage of flesh in our lives and gives us joyous obedience instead. True obedience is the fruit of the spirit, the ultimate effect of the anointing within us. Fruitfulness is God's perfect will for us in Christ Jesus.

We have been chosen to take authority over the kingdom of darkness and conquer it, with Christ radiating through us. The glory of the indwelling Christ is so bright that the devil flees from us. No weapon formed against us will prosper.[15]

In the world, our spiritual victories and excellent performance reflect the greatness of God. Jesus did not come to make us good losers but to make us winners. God is not glorified by the failure, laziness, and sloppiness of Christians whom legalism has beat down into a false humility. Instead, we must remember we are Jesus' representatives. We are His ambassadors. We have diplomatic immunity. We are heaven's outpost on earth.

Now then we are ambassadors for Christ, as though God did beseech you by us: we pray you in Christ's stead, be ye reconciled to God.[16]

We are delegates to this world from His Majesty the King of Kings. The glories of the kingdom we represent are seen in our demeanor. We are in this world yet not of this world, because there is something different within us.

Every life experience is essential for God's glory. Our total life is ordered of the Lord to teach us, to build our character, and to mature us as effective ambassadors. The heart's desire of every Christian must be to represent the kingdom of God perfectly in our sphere of influence.

We have been born from above, and it behooves us to be like the Son of God in every area of our lives. Jesus is not only the goal, He is the way. Jesus indwelling us is the pathway to victorious living here and now.

The same spirit that raised Christ from the dead dwells in us to produce Christlikeness.[17] We possess an inward potential —blood-bought, holy-ghost inspired—to attain spiritual manhood. We are pre-qualified in Christ to perform royal missions God preordained for us before He made this world. Not only do we have good news to proclaim, but also we have a glorious experience to share: Christ in us the hope of glory.[18]

> Not that we are sufficient of ourselves to think anything as of ourselves; but our sufficiency is of God.[19]

God is the source of our capabilities and abilities. We have no glory of our own. We just reflect His glory and splendor. Our sufficiency is in Him who is all-sufficient. We can do all things through Christ who strengthens us.[20]

Our divine potential is released when we humble ourselves under the mighty hand of God.[21] In Christ, humility leads to exaltation, and disappointments prove to be divine appointments. God has ordained that the new man in Christ becomes a partner, co-worker, and fellow heir with Him. As Christ died for us, we are called to recognize ourselves co-crucified, co-buried, and co-raised with Him.

Circumstances can no longer determine our lives, and flesh can no longer dominate our emotions. The Lord is our joy. Failure can no longer gain supremacy and cause us fear and defeat. Our position as victors in Christ is not contingent on whether or not we win or lose a battle. He already won the war for us.

We are already enthroned with Christ, in heavenly places far above principalities and powers.[22] We expect to win every battle, because He always leads us in triumph.[23] God has put His unbeatable Holy Spirit in us. Jesus is coming back for a victorious church.

Because He is our righteousness, our position in Christ assures us of constant victory. In him we are blameless, spotless, holy, pure, undefiled, and acceptable in the beloved.[24] We can have prevailing joy in the midst of any storm.

Our confidence is in His unconditional love for us. He will never leave us nor forsake us.[25] Our weapons for war are more than flesh, because God has made them mighty to demolish strongholds.[26] Our assurance is in the power of Jesus' blood to cleanse us from sin.[27] in God's ability to keep covenant, and the two-edged sword of "it is written" to put Satan on the run.[28]

As God's offspring in Christ, we have a birthright. We are eternal recipients of the Father's glory.

> Whereby are given unto us exceeding great and precious promises, that by these ye might be partakers of the divine nature, having escaped the corruption that is in the world through lust.[29]

The divine glory radiates from within us, because we share in His divine nature. Nature determines behavior. Birds fly and fish swim. And everything produces after its own kind. God produces after his own kind.

We love the Lord because He first loved us. He came to seek and to save us. He died that we may live. Because He lives, we can live also, and "we all with open face beholding as in a glass the glory of the Lord, are changed into the same image from glory to glory, even as by the Spirit of the Lord."[30]

Chapter 7

The Glorification of the Believer

The believer's call is unto sonship and not servanthood. The difference between servanthood and sonship is glory. Sons share in the Father's glory.

Believers need to catch a glimpse of the awesome glory we have in Christ, to be appropriated by faith. It is a privilege that can reshape our self-image and our priorities, as well as revitalizing our worship. The glory that the Father gave to Jesus is ours, since our lives are hidden in God in Christ. That abiding glory delivers us from the debilitating bondage to sin and releases us to experience unspeakable joy.

The glory of God is the manifest presence of God within us. It dispels darkness from the innermost recesses of our being. When the Lord is in His temple, all false self-reliance and security is exposed. As we gaze at Jesus, we are changed from glory to glory. The threadbare images of this world blind our eyes and prevent us from beholding the Lord. Though he is there all the time, He manifests His presence only when we seek His face.

Glorification Through Worship

Worship transforms and transfers us into heights of our manifested destiny and glory. The word "worship" comes from the Anglo-Saxon *weorthscipe,* which means "to attribute worth to an object." When we worship God, we ascribe to Him the supreme worth that is due His

40

name. Our worship is an expression of our gratitude for His choosing us to share in His glorification.

> But we speak the wisdom of God in a mystery, even the hidden wisdom, which God ordained before the world unto our glory.[1]

The gospel is the good news of our induction into the hall of fame, the glorification that God decreed before the foundation of the world for us.[2] We have been vested with the highest dignity and glory.

He purchased us in order to be a worshipping community. The act of worship brings the manifest presence of God. Jesus opened a new and living way into the holy of holies for the believers to enter into His presence. God inhabits the praises of His people. This is the highest privilege that we have as sons, because to behold the face of God and commune with Him is an inestimable blessing and delight. He imparts His glory to those who behold His glory in sweet fellowship.

> But thou, O Lord, art a shield for me; my glory, and the lifter up of mine head.[3]

Worship is a celebration of sonship. God has given us the Spirit of sonship that cries, "Abba, Father."[4] This is the Spirit that worships God through us.

"But the hour cometh, and now is, when the true worshippers shall worship the Father in spirit and in truth:"[5] This is the worship that ensures His presence. It is initiated by God's self-revelation to man, through His Son Jesus.

41

Worshipping by the spirit is an act of faith that entails a total dependence on the Holy Spirit. "For we are the circumcision, which worship God in the spirit, and rejoice in Christ Jesus, and have no confidence in the flesh."[6]

The revelation of God's unconditional love toward us produces happiness, which leads to worship as we see His presence in His sovereign act of amazing grace. The awesome majesty of God—who alone is worthy— destroys all self-confidence in the flesh. We celebrate from our hearts, because we realize that God uses His sovereignty, not to destroy us, but to remake us and to place us at the center of His glory.

Jesus came to give believers the glory of the Father, imparted to us mortals by the unconditional grace of God. He is worthy of worship because he made us worthy and acceptable into the beloved.[7]

No man had seen the full glory of God and lived, but Jesus contained the full glory of God bodily. He came to reveal that glory to us:

And the Word was made flesh, and dwelt among us, (and we beheld his glory, the glory as of the only begotten of the Father,) full of grace and truth.[8]

Who being the brightness of his glory, and the express image of his person, and upholding all things by the word of his power, when he had by himself purged our sins, sat down on the right hand of the Majesty on high.[9]

42

The more time Moses spent with God, the more he took on the glory of God. Likewise, when we behold the glory of the Father in Jesus, we are changed from one degree of glory to another. Jesus communicates God's glory to us, and we appropriate this glory into our earthen vessel.[10] This is the incredible treasure that we carry within us, that makes the devil mad.

We are beautified into His likeness by abiding in Him, John says, ". . . When he shall appear, we shall be like him; for we shall see him as he is."[11] He was made unto us sanctification and wisdom. He is our glory.

The happiness and abandonment of worship lifts us from the trivialities of everyday living to new heights of glory. When we are on our knees in worship, adoration, praise, and thanksgiving to God our Father in the wonder of our salvation, we mount up with wings like an eagle. Our glory is only the reflection of God's glory.

Our glorification is our union with God in Christ. We are partakers of the divine nature. His will has become our will, His plan our destiny, His Kingdom our Kingdom. We leave behind the wearisome pressure of living in a prodigal world. We break the gravitational pull of the externals and the temporary and move into the spiritual outer space of the heavenlies, where we are seated with Christ.

Glorification Through the Cross

We are glorified above all creation through the cross of Jesus Christ. The cross of Jesus imputed to man the

43

highest weight of glory. The Son of God exchanged His glory for our shame: He took our sins upon Himself and gave us His Father's glory.

The death of Jesus on the cross lifted man to his lost Godlike image. He died as us. He is our substitute. He is our kinsman redeemer.[12] As our kinsman redeemer he paid our debt. He gave us His riches of glory.

> What shall we then say to these things? If God be for us, who can be against us? He that spared not his own Son, but delivered him up for us all, how shall he not with him also freely give us all things?
>
> Who shall lay any thing to the charge of God's elect? It is God that justifieth. Who is he that condemneth? It is Christ that died, yea rather, that is risen again, who is even at the right hand of God, who also maketh intercession for us.
>
> Who shall separate us from the love of Christ? shall tribulation, or distress, or persecution, or famine, or nakedness, or peril, or sword? As it is written, For thy sake we are killed all the day long; we are accounted as sheep for the slaughter.
>
> Nay, in all these things we are more than conquerors through him that loved us. For I am persuaded, that neither death, nor life, nor angels, nor principalities, nor powers, nor things present, nor things to come, nor height, nor depth, nor any other creature, shall be able to separate us from

the love of God, which is in Christ Jesus our Lord." [13]

The cross of Jesus united us with Him, in death and resurrection. We are now inseparable. We are now joint-heirs with Him. Our worth is in Christ, because our new identity arises out of the death, resurrection, and glorification of Jesus.

The glorification of the believer is an accomplished fact in the cross, yet many believers for all practical purposes have "a form of godliness" without "the power thereof."[14] In so much of the Church today, the glory of God is merely a theological concept to be read about in the scriptures, with no meaning or relevance in this world. The Church is lost in a lost world. The glory is departed!

Believers in the early Church lived in constant awareness of the abiding glory in them. In so doing they provide illumination and encouragement for those of us today who seek to appropriate all that Christ achieved on Calvary on our behalf: the glory of our sonship.

Who also hath made us able ministers of the new testament; not of the letter, but of the spirit: for the letter killeth, but the spirit giveth life. But if the ministration of death, written and engraven in stones, was glorious, so that children of Israel could not steadfastly behold the face of Moses for the glory of his countenance; which glory was to be done away: How shall not the ministration of the spirit be rather glorious?[15]

45

The New Testament ministry is more beautiful than that of the Old Testament. We are partakers of unspeakable glory. The resurrection of Jesus restored to us greater glory than we lost through sin.

The excellence of glory reflected in our lives is unparalleled in history. Jesus is the glory of God, and when he abides in us, He gives us His glory. We were co-crucified with Christ and co-risen with Christ. We co-rule with Christ as co-heirs. Our holiness is the beauty of Jesus in us and through us.

> Always bearing about in the body the dying of the Lord Jesus, that the life also of Jesus might be made manifest in our body. For we which live are alway delivered unto death for Jesus' sake, that the life also of Jesus might be made manifest in our mortal flesh.[16]

As we die to the flesh, the life of Jesus is made manifest in our body. The flesh hinders the outflow of the glory of God through our lives. The scripture says, "we limited the Holy One of Israel."[17] We grieve the Spirit.[18] Like Israel of old, we limp with two opinions.[19] We are double-minded. We are unstable in all our ways.[20] We are misfocused and unglorified. Our minds need to be renewed[21] by the transforming power of the cross.

> Stand therefore, having your loins girt about with truth, and having on the breastplate of righteousness.[22]

We have a new way of thinking, because our position in creation has been changed. We have been translated from the kingdom of darkness into the Kingdom of His dear Son.[23] We are Kingdom people, kings and priests unto God. Sin displaced us in the divine economy; the blood of Jesus redeemed us and repositioned us for glory, in right standing with God. We must now think like kings, because we are now kings!

Chapter 8

Daily Victorious Walk with Jesus

Enoch walked with God: and he was not; for God took him.[1]

Enoch walked with God one day at a time. Enoch's life was not divided into spiritual and secular compartments. He walked with God no matter where he went. To him, every ground was holy ground.

David had a similar view. In Psalm 72:19, he says, "Let the whole earth be filled with thy glory." The apostle Paul explained God's nearness this way: "In him we live, and move, and have our being."[2]

Yet daily our lives repeat the story of Peter, John, and James on the Mount of Transfiguration.[3] They yearned to stay on the mountain top and separate themselves from the topsy-turvy world down in the valley, where "reality" waited for them.

For many believers, the transition from heavenly communion to the earthly hindrance of human interaction seems to require a break in their fellowship with God. However, children of God do not live in two realms, one spiritual and one secular. Instead, we "dwell in the house of the Lord for ever."[4]

We can always know the nearness of the Father, "Who hath delivered us from the power of darkness, and hath translated us into the kingdom of his dear Son."[5]

We have been transferred from the domain of darkness into God's kingdom. The continuance of sweet fellowship and communion with God depends not on externals but on the abiding, indwelling presence of God. Jesus does not remain in the closet while we venture out into the world of human realities. He said, "I will never leave thee, nor forsake thee,"[6] and "Lo, I am with you always."[7]

When we walk with God as our total sphere of influence, He guides us from victory to victory and leads us from glory to glory.

New Thinking, New Ways of Living

Every day, the man I was before I knew Christ seeks to be in control again. My old man is a legalist: he separates the spiritual from the secular. He wants to be in control of my secular world. My old man allows me to escape for a brief moment into the closet to meet with God, but he insists that I am in charge of my own world, and that I leave Jesus in the closet.

This is why so many believers live in defeat. They are deceived about who they are and where they are in Jesus. Jesus came to crucify my old man and to put him out of business forever.[8] In salvation, I am born again. I receive a new spirit and a new heart.

Salvation is a beginning, not an end, to the divine work of grace. Salvation must lead to sanctification, in

49

which God wants to transform me into the likeness of Jesus through the word, which focuses my thoughts on Jesus.

The way to defeat the old man is to mature the new man, whose impulses and desires God has re-created to be like those of Jesus. Like changing clothes, we take off the old man by putting on the new man in Christ.[9]

Our thinking determines who we are and what we do. "For as he thinketh in his heart, so is he: . . ."[10] The old man is programmed by the natural world. The new man is programmed by the word of God. The word of God transforms our stinking thinking. Paul urged the new Christians at Rome,

> I beseech you therefore, brethren, by the mercies of God, that ye present your bodies a living sacrifice, holy, acceptable unto God, which is your reasonable service. And be not conformed to this world: but be ye transformed by the renewing of your mind, that ye may prove what is that good, and acceptable, and perfect, will of God.[11]

The devil stole from Adam his Godlike mind—and image. In exchange, the serpent substituted the fruit of the knowledge of good and evil. He deceived man to believe that, by reason, it is possible to be like God, apart from God. By so doing, man took on the likeness of Satan.

But Jesus bought us and brought the divine image back to us. That new man reflects the abiding presence of the indwelling Christ. Time spent with God on Mount Horeb transformed Moses' countenance into the likeness of God.[12]

In contrast, legalism teaches people to discipline the flesh to walk in the footsteps of Jesus, but only as an imitation of Him. The tragic result is people trying to live by denying or repressing the flesh. The flesh cannot please God. The flesh cannot imitate Jesus with joy. Legalism is holiness without happiness. We are transformed into His likeness only by looking at Jesus.

It is not an achievement of our own human discipline. It requires us to recognize that our old man is crucified with Christ, and our new man is risen together with Christ and seated together with Him in heavenly places.[13]

The new man is Christ in me, the hope of glory.[14] Paul, who knew firsthand the transforming power of Jesus, wrote,

> I am crucified with Christ: nevertheless I live; yet not I, but Christ liveth in me: and the life which I now live in the flesh I live by the faith of the Son of God, who loved me, and gave himself for me.[15]

Christ in me is not something the flesh can see, yet its fruits are visible. Jesus said, "By their fruits you shall know them."[16] The fruits of the flesh are obvious, and so are the fruits of the Spirit. We do not bear fruit for Jesus. He bears fruits in us and through us. The fruits that we bear are called the fruits of the Spirit, because they are produced by the indwelling Christ.

In order for us to live out the reality of our sonship and union with Jesus in the context of our daily existence, our new man must be renewed continuously, in the knowledge of Him that called us.

51

Grace-Based Acceptance

The good news of the New Testament is God's acceptance of us—by grace alone. The words for "grace" in Hebrew are *hesed* and *hen*, undeserved love and favor. God is love, and grace is the outflowing of His love toward undeserving sinners. Grace is love in action.

The grace of God makes it possible for us to be real. We can stand before God in our fig leaves, knowing we are accepted and beloved. The grace of God does not compromise the holiness of God but provides a way out. Our election, salvation, justification, and glorification are acts of His divine initiative of grace. God unconditionally declares—

- I will forgive your iniquity.[17]

- I will remember your sins no more.[18]

- I will cleanse you.[19]

- I will give you a new heart.[20]

- I will put my spirit within you.[21]

- I will cause you to walk in my statutes.[22]

- I will never leave you.[23]

- I will never forsake you.[24]

- I will perfect that which concerns you.[25]

The grace of God cost Him His only Son. It costs to love. God fulfilled for us all the demands of holiness, and now He freely bestows on us all that Jesus is and all that He has. This is the amazing grace.

The grace of God takes care of our past sins. We are forgiven. In the present He sustains us by grace, and in the future He receives us unto Himself. Salvation, sanctification, and glorification are divine absolutes. These are divine prerogatives of grace. Our election unto Him is purely unmerited favor and grace.

Chapter 9

Satisfaction and Sanctification

Jesus is made unto us satisfaction, as well as sanctification. He is our holiness. Holiness is not a quality of our outward performance. Instead, it is the abiding presence of a holy God inside our lives. He is holy, and He imparts His holiness to us. He gives us His peace. He gives us His love. He gives us His patience. The more I yield to the lordship of Jesus, the more His life is expressed through me.

Sanctification is the satisfaction of the whole person— spirit, soul and body—by the indwelling Holy Spirit. The presence of sin is a sign of an unfulfilled soul, seeking for happiness. Human emotions crave fulfillment, but sin is like a sugary drink that never satisfies. Only one thing satisfies the yearning of the human heart: the living water that is Jesus.

Many Christians do not believe they can live a holy and happy life without compromise. The word of God clearly says, "Be ye holy; for I am holy,"[1] and without holiness "no man shall see the Lord."[2] In the hearts of those who know how deceitful the flesh is, these words produce despair. In the naive, they engender a religion

54

based upon soulish works of righteousness. But self-produced holiness is like filthy rags, in the sight of God.[3]

That kind of holiness is contrived in much hardness and heaviness. It is self-inflicted suffering for Jesus. This martyrdom syndrome of spiritual mysticism receives its reward on earth. The vanity of this soulish religion of good works is the praise of man here and now.

Laboring in the flesh, not even born-again man can attain the holiness God demands. Instead, true holiness can come only as the outward expression of the abiding presence of Jesus in us.

Freedom from Sin

Holiness is the will of God for every believer: "For this is the will of God, even your sanctification."[4]

The process of sanctification begins at the new birth and continues daily, as we decrease and Jesus increases in us. It is not our performance but the indwelling presence of the Holy Spirit that produces holiness.

Besetting sins cannot be overcome by will-power or self discipline. Jesus said, "The truth shall make you free."[5] Ignorance of the truth keeps believers in bondage to sins that will not let them alone. Thus the more truth we appropriate, the more free we become.

Truth is like light that dispels darkness. When we keep the word, the word keeps us from falling into a pit. Psalm 119:11 says, "Thy word have I hid in mine heart, that I might not sin against thee." David knew the secret of victorious living. The word held in our hearts liberates us from the shackles of sin. The apostle Paul calls the good news "the power of God unto salvation."[6]

The written word reveals the living word that sets free. By itself, the letter of the law kills. But we receive spiritual life by seeking the communication that God continually makes available to us. Jesus said, "Man shall not live by bread alone, but by every word that proceedeth out of the mouth of God."[7]

The living word is the *rhema* that is imparted by the Holy Spirit. It is a personalized word to you, in your immediate situation. It is a practical word, one you must hear and do. ". . . Be ye doers of the word, and not hearers only, deceiving your own selves."[8] The living word is not just for thinking about, but for doing.

Self-deception is listening only to your flesh, rather than acting upon the word by faith. Jesus told the people,

> Not everyone that saith unto me, Lord, Lord, shall enter into the kingdom of heaven; but he that doeth the will of my Father which is in heaven. . . .Therefore whosoever heareth these sayings of mine, and doeth them, I will liken him unto a wise man, which built his house upon a rock: . . . [9]

True and lasting spiritual foundation is acting upon the word against the dictates of the flesh or evidence to the contrary. It is as hard as digging unto solid rock. God does not make it easy for the flesh to obey God. Flesh must be crucified. But when we are near to Christ, it is easy to do God's will.

Holy Spirit and Happiness

God's eternal plan for us is joy unspeakable. In order to accomplish and guarantee that plan, the sovereignty of God foreordained every event in our lives. The devil designed for us a cruel alternative program. But his scheming was in vain, because God sent Jesus. ". . . For this purpose the Son of God was manifested, that he might destroy the works of the devil."[10]

When Jesus returned to heaven, God sent the Holy Spirit to carry out His sovereign will of joy unspeakable, full of glory,[11] in and through us. The devil is active in our world, seeking whom he may devour[12] and causing all suffering. Sufferings are satanic interferences in our lives.

The word tells us that God does not send suffering to His beloved children. On the contrary, He blesses them. "Every good gift and every perfect gift is from above, and cometh down from the Father of lights, with whom is no variableness, neither shadow of turning."[13]

Everything beautiful that comes from above is communicated and imparted to us by the Holy Spirit. The Holy Spirit gives us beauty for ashes and a garment of praise for the spirit of heaviness.[14] He is our Comforter.[15]

The Holy Spirit abides with us in order to expedite the Father's will for our lives. It is not incumbent upon flesh to do God's will. It is too good for flesh to comprehend and impossible for flesh to accomplish. Only absolute surrender to the Holy Spirit leads to the absolute happiness of experiencing God's power.

The devil is always present to deceive us into missing God's plan. Yet the sovereignty of God takes our suffering, caused by Satan and disobedience, and utilizes it to teach us to fear the Lord, bringing glory to His name.

This is why the apostle Paul says, "And we know that all things work together for good to them that love God, to them who are the called according to his purpose." [16]

Jesus came to demonstrate that when you love God and walk with Him all things do work together for good. The happiness of Jesus on earth was from knowing God was in immediate control. Daily, the Holy Spirit brings harmony to our souls by reminding us of the Father's unconditional love and presence.

Jesus prayed that we might partake of His joy, which came from absolute obedience to the Father. ". . . That my joy might remain in you, and that your joy might be full."[17]

The joy of Jesus was daily intimacy with the Father, realized through the Holy Spirit during His earthly ministry. The believer's destined end is not service to God, but holiness and happiness as the Holy Ghost makes us aware of God's presence in our lives.

We can endure the turmoil of life because of the indwelling presence of the Holy Spirit, who lifts us above circumstances. The sovereignty of God assures us that God anticipated every situation we are going through.

Even before we see the victory, He has made available to us His grace sufficient to rejoice.

The Holy Spirit continually communicates to us the Father's unconditional love that produces in us unconditional joy. "If God be for us, who can be against us?"[18]

When we behold our beloved Father, we are liberated from the beggarly elements of performance and law.[19] Love removes the risk of failure. God is love![20] The Holy Spirit is love! Jesus is love! We are the object of unfathomable love.[21]

The Holy Spirit gives us the revelation of God's infinite love and interprets to us the will of God for our eternal happiness in Jesus. That happiness is not just a future reality but something to be received and enjoyed now.

The New Testament believers' experience was stamped with the hallmark of joy in adversity. This supernatural lifestyle of joy unspeakable, full of glory, emanated from the revelation that their bodies were the temple of the Holy Spirit. Our intimacy and union with God transforms us into the image of Jesus and fills us with abundant joy.

Chapter 10

Sanctification

Sanctification is the daily cleansing of the believer. This process takes place as we empty ourselves of the world and allow ourselves to be filled with more of the Lord. The degree of our yieldedness and surrender to the Lord determines the degree of our sanctification. We are not a source of holiness; we are containers of the Lord's holiness that He imparts to us.

The center point of our redemption is the restoration of our Godlike image in Jesus. We reflect like the moon the glory of the sun of righteousness. The darkness of depression, anxiety, fear, and doubt is dispelled by the presence of God in us.

The temple was made holy by the presence of God. In the same way, what makes us holy is Who abides inside us, not what we do.

He purchased us in order to fill us up with His glory. Our outward holiness is the overflow of the abiding glory in our inner being. That glory within gives us wholeness or *shalom*, a Hebrew word meaning perfect well-being of spirit, soul, and body.

Man-made holiness, whether Catholic works or evangelical discipline, is a contrived outward

60

performance that lacks the "joy unspeakable and full of glory" that Peter talks about.[1] Will-religion produces holiness by suppressing the flesh. This quality of man-made holiness is devoid of happiness and fulfillment. It is sacrifice without satisfaction.

Legalism is externalism and self-righteousness. It requires incredible human will to deny the flesh. This explains why self-righteous people are miserable. They carry the cross but never want to die on it.

> I am crucified with Christ: nevertheless I live; yet not I, but Christ liveth in me: and the life which I now live in the flesh I live by the faith of the Son of God, who loved me, and gave himself for me.[2]

Until you die on the cross, you will never experience the resurrection life. We take our cross and follow Jesus to Calvary, where we are crucified with Him. We are buried with Him. We are risen with Him. We are ascended to the right hand of God with Him. We are seated together with Him in heavenly places. We are ruling and reigning together with Him. Soulish Saul had to be transformed to Paul before he could say, "For me to live is Christ."[3]

Our sanctification is mediated to our souls by the word. Jesus said, "The truth shall set you free."[4] The truth or the word tells you who you are in Christ and what you have in Christ. We are the righteousness of God in Christ. Our obedience is wrought of God.

Jesus brought holiness to us. He exchanged His holiness for our sinfulness: "For he hath made him to be sin for us, who knew no sin; that we might be made the righteousness of God in him."[5]

In the Old Testament, the law demanded of my flesh sinless perfection. But it was to no avail, because the law of sin and death kept me in bondage to sin. It is like the law of gravity; it keeps us tied down to sin. Jesus came to establish a new law of life in Him, which works like the law of aerodynamics so we can soar with God to new heights of glory.

"For the law of the Spirit of life in Christ Jesus hath made me free from the law of sin and death."[6] The law of the spirit of life, which sets us free, is Christ in us, the hope of glory. He gives the vision and the provision. He is in us to will and to do of His good pleasure.[7]

He doesn't just give us direction; He transports us through enemy territory, fortifying and arming and preserving us as though we were in a tank. The apostle Paul says, "He always causes us to triumph."[8] The battle is not ours. The battle is the Lord's.[9] Our victory is guaranteed by God Almighty. We do not have to read the last chapter to know that we win. Every page says we win.

The law no longer condemns me but now describes the new me in Christ. My old man is dead to the beggarly elements of the law.[10] Now, for me to live is Christ and to die is gain.[11] I am dead to the world. I no longer live by reason or sight, but by every word that proceeds from the mouth of God.[12] Our joy is not in knowing that at the end we will win the war, but that we win each battle, because He always leads us to triumph.

David overcame the world by keeping the word. When you keep the word, the word will keep you. The Holy Spirit activates the word, actualizing the will of God in our lives. The commandment of God becomes the promise of what He intends to establish in our lives.

There is power in the word, because God stands behind it to fulfill it. He told Jeremiah,"I will hasten my word to perform it."[13]

The word is God's promissory note, to be honored on sight when presented to the Bank of Heaven in Jesus' name. God guarantees all the promises in the word. His promises are irrevocable and eternal: "Heaven and earth shall pass away, but my words shall not pass away."[14]

David had a revelation of the power of the word to sustain him from evil. He depended on the word for victory. He claimed the word.

Holiness is born in us by the word. Jesus said, "My word has made thee clean." Jesus came to give heaven's joy and life to His disciples: "The thief cometh not, but for to steal, and to kill, and to destroy: I am come that they might have life, and that they might have it more abundantly."[15]

The word is the substance of unseen things, just like a certificate of deposit. When you take your money to the bank, you cease to see it. You put all your trust into the certificate of deposit, a piece of paper they give you. You believe your money is safe and growing, and you do not have sleepless nights worrying about it.

We have something in the word greater than any bank in the world. The word of God is a negotiable instrument. It is the most viable thing you have in time and eternity. You can draw on it at any time. The word is sufficient for all your needs.

The tragedy in the body of Christ is that charismatics seek after experiences, and evangelicals seek after knowledge, but God is revealed in His word. Believe the word, act on the word, and you will see the glory of God. You do not need to pursue mystical experiences or knowledge. God is in His word.

But the righteousness which is of faith speaketh on this wise, Say not in thine heart, Who shall ascend into heaven? (that is, to bring Christ down from above:)

Or, Who shall descend into the deep? (that is, to bring Christ again from the dead.)

But what saith it? The word is nigh thee, even in thy mouth, and in thy heart: that is, the word of faith, which we preach; . . . [16]

The word is the seed of holiness and happiness. The word is the seed of righteousness. The word is the seed of joy unspeakable and full of glory. The word is the seed of prosperity. The word is the seed of victory.

"Thy word have I hid in mine heart that I might not sin against thee."[17] Fruit comes not from the soil but from the seed. The word is the seed, and we are the soil. There is no growth where there is no seed. God has limited Himself to His word, and He will perform it. The word in your mouth is all it takes for a miracle to take place. Take God at His word. God is the DNA in the seed or word.

We are the field where God wants to plant the word. God's seed grows only in good soil that has been broken and watered with prayer. Every seed produces after its own kind. The word of God produces in us the heavenly fruit of love, joy, peace, long-suffering, gentleness, goodness, faith, meekness, and temperance.[18] But flesh produces after its own kind: holiness without happiness.

The word speaks of men "having a form of godliness, but denying the power thereof."[19] They have a "Baptist form," "charismatic form," "Catholic form," or other form of holiness that lacks the reality of the abiding Holy Spirit.

They are lukewarm because they are too busy fighting the flesh. They are miserable because they are holding down their emotions. Self-righteousness often produces a critical and judgmental spirit. Good self-righteous people are like Job's friends. They have all the right answers, but they do not know God. Their righteousness is born out of self determination and the beggarly elements of the law. The letter of the law killeth.[20]

As the temple was made holy by the presence of God, so are we made holy by His abiding presence in us. The Lord is our righteousness.

> In his days Judah shall be saved, and Israel shall dwell safely: and this is his name whereby he shall be called, THE LORD OUR RIGHTEOUS-NESS.[21]

Holiness is being wholly controlled by the Holy Spirit. We do not keep God; He keeps us. We don't restrain from evil ourselves, but the Lord delivers us from evil. The Lord taught His disciples to pray, "Deliver us from evil: For thine is the kingdom, and the power, and the glory." He delivers us from evil daily. We are His workmanship, created unto good works.[22] The just shall live by faith, in the faithfulness of God.[23] He is the author and finisher of our faith.[24]

The sovereign purpose of redemption was to reclaim us as vessels of His glory[25]—to indwell us. As purchased property, God has total rights over our lives. He has the title deed to all that I am and to all that I have. The depth of my union with Him is the depth of my holiness.

Holiness is not an infusion of grace, but an abiding presence of God in my heart. "Be ye holy; for I am holy"[26] is a sovereign invitation to make ourselves available for Him to dwell in us and to impart His holiness to us. The more I let go of the flesh and surrender to Him, the more I receive His holiness.

Jesus taught His disciples to pray, "Thy will be done on earth, as it is in heaven."[27] God wants us to pray for His perfect will on earth to be done in our lives, as it is in heaven. Heaven is in harmony with the divine will. Holiness is the will of God being done in our lives, in the context of daily living in this topsy-turvy world.

There is a sovereign purpose to our lives. God wants us to yield our lives to Him, so that He can demonstrate His will to the world. The will of God is not something we do for God, because we are called not to servanthood but to sonship. The will of God is "that we may know him."[28] The Father wants to have intimacy with us. The Father wants us to abide in Him.

Jesus came to demonstrate what it is to be a son of God. He walked with God. He said, "The Father that dwelleth in me, he doeth the works."[29] The will of God for us is being home with Dad in the Father's house. David said,"I will dwell in the house of the Lord for ever."[30] This is why God called him the man after His own heart.[31]

The prodigal son did not want to stay home, because he did not understand the love of his father.[32] He felt cheated. Though his body was home, his heart was gone with the wind. He soon followed his heart, like most unfulfilled Christians. It is not long before they compromise themselves to the world.

Every sin is a dissatisfaction with the Father. It is a quest for fulfillment apart from the Father. The prodigal son was self-righteous, to the extent that he requested his rightful inheritance and left home. For a while he felt good doing things his own way, until the bottom fell out. Life has a way of driving us back home to the Father's house, because nothing in this world can fulfill us except Jesus. He is all that we need.

At our Father's house, it is partying every day. Holiness is happiness. It is abundant life. It is joy unspeakable. It is peace that passes all understanding.[33] It is heaven all the way to heaven. It is a love affair with Jesus.

Chapter 11

The Sovereignty of God in Prayer

Many believers question the purpose of prayer. If God preordained everything before the foundation of this world, and His will is going to be done willy nilly, why pray? Is prayer just a meaningless exercise? How do God's sovereignty and our prayer work together?

God ordained prayer as a means of grace to bring His sovereign will to pass in our lives. Jesus prayed the will of God to be done, and He taught His disciples to pray. Prayer does not change God's mind, but it realigns man with His perfect will.

The purposes of God established before the foundation of this world are unchangeable. That unchangeability of God's sovereign will is the source of the believer's blessed assurance and eternal security, "For the gifts and calling of God are without repentance."[1]

God's sovereign will was actualized in Christ Jesus. He fulfilled all of God's holy demands and obtained for us an eternal inheritance in Him.

In whom also we have obtained an inheritance, being predestinated according to the purpose of him who worketh all things after the counsel of his own will.[2]

68

Through His death and resurrection, He raised us up together with Him and seated us together with Him in heavenly places,[3] making available to us all things.

> According as his divine power hath given unto us all things that pertain unto life and godliness, through the knowledge of him that hath called us to glory and virtue: Whereby are given unto us exceeding great and precious promises: that by these ye might be partakers of the divine nature, having escaped the corruption that is in the world though lust.[4]

The sovereignty of God made available to us everything that we need for life and godliness in Christ, to be appropriated by our prayers. Prayer is abandonment to God's will. It is agreeing with God. It is a humble submission to His sovereign will. God's will is to meet all our needs according to His glory.[5]

"For your Father knoweth what things ye have need of, before ye ask him ."[6] God anticipated every situation and made total provision, to be received by prayer and thanksgiving. The Word tells us the will of God, so that we can pray according to His will. When we do, He answers us: "If we ask any thing according to his will, he heareth us."[7]

God made total provision for Adam's happiness before He made Adam. In the same way, He knew us and provided for us before we were born.[8] Our happiness is found in complete harmony with God's will for our lives. Prayer relies on the steadfastness of God's love towards His children. There is tremendous joy in knowing that His sovereign will is based upon His prior knowledge of us in Christ, acceptable in the beloved.

> For I know the thoughts that I think toward you, saith the Lord, thoughts of peace, and not of evil, to give you an expected end.[9]

Prayer positions us to receive all that God has prepared for us in love, before the foundation of this world. God's will for us is to enjoy life to the fullest. Jesus came that we may have abundant life.[10] He demonstrated by His life how to live at the center of God's will every day. How to delight in doing His will. How to pray according to God's will. How to receive answers to every prayer.

Prayer is God's way of solving every problem. God turns every problem into a blessing when we pray, because He desires our happiness. God is on our side, and Jesus came to demonstrate that fact beyond any shadow of doubt. Calvary is God's ultimate demonstration of His love towards us.

The Almighty uses His might to defeat our enemies. The foreknowledge of God turns everything the devil meant for evil into a blessing, because God outsmarts the devil. My heavenly Dad already expected every one of Satan's surprise attacks on my life and made provision for my victory. Christ leads us from victory to victory by using His sovereignty to overrule the devil, in order to bless us in every situation.

The devil, on the other hand, appeals to our old man and quickens the lusts of the flesh, to fight against our spirit man in vain, because Christ is in me to will and to do of His good pleasure. He attempts to deceive us into living by sight and not by faith, by reason and not by the Word, hoping to enslave us again.

As we turn our eyes upon Jesus, victory is instant. Total surrender to the sovereign will of God leads to total victory. Jesus trusted the Father completely, even unto death on the cross. He had total faith in His father's perfect will. He endured the cross for the joy that was set before Him:[11] the joy of pleasing the Father.

Chapter 12

The Fulfillment of God's Will

Thy will be done on earth, as it is in heaven.[1]

Redemption realigns us with God's plan for the ages. For each one of us, there is a unique place in the divine economy that no one else can fill. We are re-created in Christ Jesus to accomplish the high calling upon our lives that God purposed from the foundation of the ages, "For we are his workmanship, created in Christ Jesus unto good works, which God hath before ordained that we should walk in them."[2] God wants to display his glory by demonstrating through us His rule over the principalities and powers of darkness.

On Calvary's cross, Jesus stripped the devil of control, once and for all. All power and authority have been given to Jesus, in heaven and on earth. Every demon flees at the mention of His name. That means the devil can no longer stop the children of God from doing the will of God. Jesus said, "I will build my church; and the gates of hell shall not prevail against it."[3]

God's plan for our lives is unstoppable. There are not enough demons in hell to hinder us from pressing on toward the mark of the high calling of God. Therefore, the will of God will be done on earth as it is in heaven. God's original intent is being fulfilled in our lives today. For His pleasure we were created!

God has put His Spirit in our hearts to weave us into the tapestry of His will. The steps of a righteous man are ordered of the Lord,[4] so that He can lead us from victory to victory and from faith to faith. Defeat and failure come when we order our own steps.

The common problem in the body of Christ is that most Christians live by common sense, and not by the word. Jesus defeated Satan by using the word. We defeat Satan in the same way!

Our carnal will leads us astray. Will-religion in its self-righteousness prays to God to bless its own plan and invites God to come for a ride, and to help out when things get hard.

The problem is that God never comes with us for a ride. He demands that we go with Him. Jesus said, "Come, follow me."[5] To walk with God is to go with God, where *He* is going. He will not go with us where we are going.

He demands absolute surrender. Self-will must be crucified. God doesn't want our capability but our availability. He will not accept the fruit of human labor or share His glory. The will of God for our lives is not realized by human struggle. He sent an angel to make that clear to Zechariah:

> Then he answered and spake unto me, saying, this is the word of the Lord unto Zerubbabel, saying, Not by might, nor by power, but by my spirit, saith the Lord of hosts.[6]

Our call is to sonship and intimacy with the Father. Our union with the Father enables Him to fulfill His will in our lives. The Father works all things in our lives after the counsel of His own will, making us perfect in every good work that is pleasing in His sight.[7] The only pressure He puts on us is to let go and let God have His way, which is for our greatest benefit.

Our new man is created after His likeness, and so we naturally desire to be in complete harmony with the Father. The will of God is being done on earth as it is in heaven, in us and through us, as we abide in Him.

We seek Jesus to abide in us, because Christ in us is our salvation, and Christ through us is our fruit. Obedience flows from that intimacy. Jesus was able to say that He delighted to do His Father's works, because the Father dwelled in Him.[8]

The will of God is easy, as long as God does it. It is impossible for the flesh to do it. Many Christians begin in the Spirit, but then they get bewitched by the beggarly elements of the law.[9] The law puts pressure on the flesh to perform and to do good works. Discipline produces not holiness but self-righteousness.

Before we can experience resurrection life, flesh must die. We must unplug all artificial life-support systems that are keeping us alive. However, the glory awaiting us after death to the flesh cannot be compared with the joy of being raised up with Christ.

We must guard against letting our thinking and actions be influenced by our circumstances, rather than the word of God. Many times externals contradict the word of God. For instance, when in the natural I see lack, I panic and fall apart, but then I look to Jesus. The word tells me; "Your needs are met according to his riches in glory."[10] What do I believe, my situation or God's promise?

When I feel down and defeated, the word says to me, "You are more than a conqueror through him that loved you."[11] When I feel worthless, the word tells me, "I can do all things through Christ who strengthens me."[12] When I feel abandoned and lonely, the word says, "I will never leave you nor forsake you."[13] When it looks impossible, Jesus says, "All things are possible to him that believes."[14]

I have a daily choice: whether to believe God or my circumstances. I can walk by sight or by faith.[15] To enable me to walk by faith, my mind has to be renewed every day by the word, which reveals the will of God. I must choose either to believe it or to doubt. When I believe the word, the will of God is done in my life as it is done in heaven.

Jesus died to redeem me from the curse of the law.[16] He made available to me all the riches of heaven in Christ Jesus.[17] All that Jesus has, I have, and all that Jesus is, I am in Him. The apostle Paul says, "Not I, but Christ liveth in me."[18]

Being in Christ, my soul is satisfied and my mind is renewed daily. The character of Jesus and his resurrection power and glory become manifest in me, according to the degree that I am yielded to His Lordship.

Doing the will of God militates against the flesh, the world, and the devil. Like Joshua of old, it is taking the land from the giants. It is an act of holy boldness.

We possess the land by a walk of faith. We are to give all diligence to enter into the realm of the Spirit, which constitutes our real heritage. Truly the Lord has prepared great and mighty things for his people:

> Eye hath not seen, nor ear heard, neither have entered into the heart of man, the things which God hath prepared for them that love him.[19]

> In whom we have redemption through his blood, the forgiveness of sins, according to the riches of his grace; Wherein he hath abounded toward us in all wisdom and prudence; . . .[20]

The will of God is to arm us to take the promised land of spiritual power and authority. God has willed the land to us, and the devil's occupation is illegal. The spiritual battle has been fought and victory won on Calvary's cross for you and me. We take the land only by dying to self and remaining in the One who defeated Satan once and for all. When we come in Jesus' name, spiritual wickedness in heavenly places flees.

The will of God is to mature us into His likeness.

> For the perfecting of the saints, for the work of the ministry, for the edifying of of the body of Christ: Till we all come in the unity of the faith, and of the knowledge of the Son of God, unto a perfect man, unto the measure of the stature of the fulness of Christ: . . .[21]

God wants to lead his people onward to greater heights and greater depths of His infinite glory. No child of God should be content with a marginal life; instead, we must press on and appropriate all that the Lord has for us in Christ Jesus.

Chapter 13

Glorification Through Suffering

As children of God we are beautified and glorified through suffering. James wrote, "My brethren, count it all joy when ye fall into divers temptations; Knowing this, that the trying of your faith worketh patience."[1]

Pressure makes the image of Christ indelible upon us. A stone-cutter uses compressed air to blow sand on a block of granite until the design is perfectly etched into the stone. The devil, not God, is the source of all suffering. In every situation, what the devil meant for evil God uses to beautify and to perfect the image of His Son upon us.

Suffering sharpens the quality of our spiritual sensitivity. The scripture says that Jesus learned obedience through the things he suffered.[2] Persecution is the universal result of the manifested power of God. All the prophets were persecuted for their faithfulness. The apostles were martyred for their testimony.

However, not all suffering glorifies God. Only when we suffer for His name's sake is it glorifying to God.

Blessed are they which are persecuted for righteousness' sake: for theirs is the kingdom of heaven. Blessed are ye, when men shall revile

78

you, and persecute you, and shall say all manner of evil against you falsely, for my sake. Rejoice, and be exceeding glad: for great is your reward in heaven: for so persecuted they the prophets which were before you.[3]

The blessedness of suffering for Jesus is not in the suffering itself but in the testing of our faith, which is more precious than gold. Our glorification is in our deliverance by the sovereignty of God. Paul assured the believers, "Now thanks be unto God, which always causeth us to triumph in Christ, and maketh manifest the savour of his knowledge by us in every place."[4]

Our lives are enriched by the things we suffer for Jesus out of obedience to His word and will. Suffering reveals the heart. Jesus said that the prince of this world had no power over Him.[5] That was because the devil cannot control where there is no sin.

Suffering will produce in us only a more Christlike image. When suffering is for righteousness' sake, it brings glory to God.

Jesus' suffering was in total obedience to the Father's will. Unfortunately, much of the suffering in the body of Christ is born of disobedience and walking in the flesh. We also bring suffering upon ourselves by not seeking the will of God. Doing our own thing has consequences, and missing God always leads to misfortune. Self-control leads to self-destruction, if it does not spring from the a desire to obey the Lord. A believer should be Spirit-controlled and Spirit-led.

All human plans are in conflict with God's plan. His thoughts are not our thoughts, and His ways are not our ways.[6] Jesus suffered for daily obeying His Father, with whom He was in constant fellowship. He delighted in doing the will of Him that sent Him,[7] in spite of the opposition.

Moses suffered for doing the will of his God. The children of Israel rebelled against him, but he did not rebel against his God. Daniel was thrown into the lion's den for his God. The three Hebrew children were thrown into the furnace for the sake of their God. Jeremiah was put into the well for being faithful to God. All the prophets suffered death for being faithful to God.

The apostles were martyred for the sake of the gospel. Paul was subject to much suffering in each city, for being faithful to the call of God upon his life. God is always glorified when we suffer for him. God gives us grace to endure and to overcome.

And he said unto me, My grace is sufficient for thee: for my strength is made perfect in weakness. Most gladly therefore will I rather glory in my infirmities, that the power of Christ may rest upon me.[8]

Our God reigns. For our blessing He overturns Satan's desires and his plan to destroy us. "And we know that all things work together for good to them that love God, to them who are the called according to his purpose."[9]

What is the good that comes out of suffering? How can suffering be a blessing? Common sense cannot realize by analysis the purpose of suffering. We walk not by sight but by faith. The just shall live by faith. Our faith is tried by the fire of suffering and made pure like gold.

> My brethren, count it all joy when ye fall into divers temptations; Knowing this, that the trying of your faith worketh patience. But let patience have her perfect work, that ye may be perfect and entire, wanting nothing.[10]

Jesus won the victory for us. The devil comes to test our faith in our salvation as a finished work. He wants us to lose sight of the fact that he is defeated and that he has no power over us.

Suffering procures *hypomone*, translated "patience," which actually means "endurance" or "perseverance." We endure because we have been endued by power from on high.[11] The divine preservation enables us to keep going to the end, until patience has her perfect work, that we may be perfect and entire, wanting nothing.

> For it is God which worketh in you both to will and to do of his good pleasure.[12]

> Now the God of peace, that brought again from the dead our Lord Jesus, that great shepherd of the sheep, through the blood of the everlasting covenant, Make you perfect in every good work to do his will, working in you that which is wellpleasing in his sight, through Jesus Christ; to whom be glory for ever and ever. Amen.[13]

> Now unto him that is able to keep you from falling, and to present you faultless before the

presence of his glory with exceeding joy, To the only wise God our Saviour, be glory and majesty, dominion and power, both now and for ever. Amen.[14]

The Lord knoweth how to deliver the godly out of temptations.[15]

It is a false assumption that we can engage the devil in spiritual combat and win. The battle is not ours.[16] We do not keep God, he keeps us. He preserves us until the day of the Lord Jesus.[17] Therefore, what the devil meant for evil, God turns around for our blessing. He turns our sorrow into happiness.

Every attack of Satan is God's opportunity to demonstrate His love towards His children. The sovereignty of God preserves us from falling and instead vindicates us and glorifies Himself through us. We are the glory of God on earth. Through us, He shows his immutable power and unsearchable wisdom to the principalities and powers of darkness. He defeated Satan on Calvary, and He is demonstrating it throughout the ages through His elect. When the devil wants us to suffer, he always suffers defeat instead. We are more than conquerors through Christ.[18]

Glorification Through Prosperity

Jesus restored to us our lost dominion. The Holy Spirit energizes redeemed man to fulfill God's original plan of ruling this universe through a man like Himself. Adam was created in the image of God to have dominion on the earth. We are re-made into the image of God in Christ Jesus our Lord, to reign with Him. Jesus is King of kings and Lord of lords. We are kings and priests unto our God.[19]

We have absolute assurance of victory in our divine mission on earth, because He has received all power in heaven and earth, and He promised He will be with us until the end of the age.[20] This promise was made to a small group who were persecuted by their own countrymen and opposed by the mightiest men of the most powerful empire in history. They were outnumbered, outgunned, and outsmarted. They did not have a chance to survive. Yet the Church came out triumphant and victorious, a clear winner over Jerusalem and Rome.

The gates of hell will not prevail against the people of God.[21] In the second Adam, man regained his dominion over the powers of darkness and the earth.[22] The lost kingship has been restored to the elect of God.

Jesus defeated Satan once and for all. The gates of hell collapsed, and Jesus triumphed over hell. The fact that Jesus is now King of kings is precisely the reason we have confidence to spoil Satan's kingdom. Jesus said, "How can one enter into a strong man's house, and spoil his goods, except he first bind the strong man? and then he will spoil his house."[23]

Jesus bound the strong man Satan, in order that we could plunder his house and carry off his goods. The apostle Paul said the Lord Jesus disarmed the rulers and authorities, in triumph making a public display of them.[24] Satan was rendered powerless and useless [25]

Jesus came to bind the devil and render him powerless to keep him from spoiling his house. Satan now flees from us when we resist him.[26] He has no power except what we give him.

The problem today is the theology of defeat. For too long, believers have been characterized by despair and retreat. Christians expect to lose it all to the devil and then "rapture out" in defeat. This is not the blessed hope. It is the apostasy of the church, which will bring the darkest hour in history.

Christians have been conditioned by the theology of defeat to allow the devil to illegally occupy territory that Jesus liberated. He gave us the command, "Occupy till I come."[27] We are to maintain the victory that Jesus won on Calvary, yet Christians are steadily giving up ground to the enemy. What we believe determines what we do. Most Christians believe it is too late to win.

The word tells us, "Where there is no vision, the people perish."[28] The children of God no longer have a vision. The theology of defeat is Satan's endgame strategy to discourage the saints from standing up in the public square for Jesus. The Lord wants us to have dominion on the earth until He comes. The despair and pessimism that characterize the church today indicate the effects of the Church's bewitchment by the other gospel: the gospel of defeatism, escapism, and rapturism.

I believe in the eschatology of triumph. The imminent return of Jesus is no reason to retreat and withdraw from life. It is a reason to occupy and have dominion on the earth till he comes. God is glorified only through our victory. Jesus won the game for us. The strong man is bound. We must spoil his house in this terminal generation.

Glorification Through Covenantal Relationship

Our blessings are not conditional but covenantal. We are not under the law but under grace. In Christ, we are the children of Abraham. We are co-heirs with Christ of all the unconditional and eternal blessings that God gave to Abraham.

> Now the Lord had said unto Abram, Get thee out of thy country, and from thy kindred, and from thy father's house, unto a land that I will shew thee: And I will make of thee a great nation, and I will bless thee, and make thy name great; and thou shalt be a blessing: And I will bless them that bless thee, and curse him that curseth thee: and in thee shall all families of the earth be blessed.[29]

> After these things the word of the Lord came unto Abram in a vision, saying, Fear not, Abram: I am thy shield, and thy exceeding great reward.[30]

God made a one-sided commitment to bless Abraham spiritually and materially. It was a covenant that glorified and exalted Abraham. The sign to the world that God was with Abraham was going to be divine blessings and divine protection.

You are as big as your God. You are as powerful as your God. The Lord said to Abraham, "I am going to make you big." Our bigness reflects the bigness of our God.

Abraham had faith in God. He trusted God. He rested in God. He rejoiced in God. He obeyed God. He worshipped God. He did not allow his possessions to possess him. He looked for a city whose builder and maker is God,[31] not as an escape from misery. Abraham was in love with God. He did not seek gifts from God, but he sought for God Himself. Abraham was willing to give up his best, his only begotten son, for his God.

Abraham's external prosperity signified his love affair with God. We are destined for greatness apart from human performance. All that we are and all that we have are inherent in our covenantal relationship with God in Christ Jesus.

The new covenant embodies and consummates all the past covenants. All the other covenants were in anticipation of the Messianic covenant, the last covenant. This covenant of grace grants us unsearchable riches in Christ. Like Abraham of old, we can know the Lord is our shield and exceeding great reward. Abraham believed the covenant. He rejoiced in it! He depended on it! He waited on it! The covenant radicalized his life. It prospered him beyond measure.

And Abram was very rich in cattle, in silver, and in gold. [32]

Glorification Through Soul Prosperity

The state of our soul dictates how we feel and what we do each day. The soul controls our will, mind, and emotions. God wants our soul state to be in harmony with His Spirit: "Beloved, I wish above all things that thou mayest prosper and be in health, even as thy soul prospereth."[33]

The Greek verb *euodoo* is compounded of *eu*, "well," and *hodos*, "way," which originally meant "have a prosperous journey." It was metaphorically used to mean "prosper." God wants all things to go *eu*, well, for us, even as our soul goes *eu*, well.

"Be in health" comes from the Greek word *hygiainein*, which means "be sound and healthy." When the soul is on sound and healthy terms with the Lord, our bodies will automatically line up with our inner being in perfect harmony. The Hebrew word *shalom*, which meant "perfect well-being," best explains what happens when we are in divine order.

David understood that soul prosperity is the key to material prosperity and victorious living:

> Blessed is the man that walketh not in the counsel of the ungodly, nor standeth in the way of sinners, nor sitteth in the seat of the scornful. But his delight is in the law of the Lord; and in his law doth he meditate day and night. And he shall be like a tree planted by the rivers of water, that bringeth forth his fruit in his season; his leaf also shall not wither; and whatsoever he doeth shall prosper.[34]

Meditation on the word transforms the soul, renews the mind, strengthens the will, and gladdens the emotions. Happy people are holy and productive. Meditation on the word ensures divine prosperity of the whole man—spirit, soul, and body. Total prosperity. God told Joshua that for daily victory the secret was daily meditation on the word.

This book of the law shall not depart out of thy mouth; but thou shalt meditate therein day and night, that thou mayest observe to do according to all that is written therein: for then thou shalt make they way prosperous, and then thou shalt have good success.[35]

God wants his people successful. He created us to have dominion. He restored authority to us through Christ's death and resurrection. The word gives us the true picture of who we are in Christ and what we have in Him. Meditation on the word empowers us to take our rightful place of authority and dominion.

Jesus did not come to make good losers out of us. The theology of defeat opiates people to accept misery as a sign of spirituality. Jesus never taught defeatism: "But seek ye first the kingdom of God, and his righteousness; and all these things shall be added unto you."[36]

Jesus taught people how to obtain power to prosper by seeking first the King, who gives to His sheep the kingdom and all the other things. He told them, "Fear not, little flock; for it is your Father's good pleasure to give you the kingdom."[37]

Jesus never said that if you seek the kingdom all these other things will be added when you die. Because Jesus wants His children to have dominion on earth, He has made us kings and priests unto God. We are kings. We think like kings, we act like kings, we rule like kings, because the Kingdom of God is in us. We are already seated with Christ in heavenly places.[38]

The disciples wanted to know whether following Jesus meant they were destined for poverty and misery in this life and joy hereafter in heaven. Jesus, who taught denying oneself and following Him, clearly rejected the theology of defeat.

> But he shall receive an hundredfold now in this time, houses, and brethren, and sisters, and mothers, and children, and lands, with persecutions; and in the world to come eternal life.[39]

He assured his disciples that what they gave up would be returned one hundred times over in this life. They did not have to wait for the rapture to be blessed. People would be jealous and persecute them, not for being miserable for Jesus, but for being blessed. Jesus taught his disciples to expect big things in this life. He came to restore man's lost dominion. He came to give us abundant life.

> The thief cometh not, but for to steal, and to kill, and to destroy: I am come that they might have life, and that they might have it more abundantly.[40]

Abundant life begins in the heart and flows out into every dimension of human existence. Jesus is our all in all. He is all we need for prosperity and fulfillment. Our glorification is not some future event. We already have the treasure in an earthen vessel.[41] Justification puts us in right standing with God, and sanctification—seeking first the kingdom of God and His righteousness—positions us to receive a hundredfold in this life.

Prosperity without holiness or without soul prosperity is death. Possessions have a way of possessing the soul that is not sanctified. God chose Israel for blessings, but the secret was in following the laws of God. These dominion laws open God's treasure house.

Deuteronomy 28:1-13 names the conditions and lists the rewards of walking in God's ways.

And it shall come to pass, if thou shalt hearken diligently unto the voice of the Lord thy God, to observe and to do all his commandments which I command thee this day, that the Lord thy God will set thee on high above all nations of the earth: And all these blessings shall come on thee, and overtake thee, if thou shalt hearken unto the voice of the Lord thy God.

Blessed shalt thou be in the city, and blessed shalt thou be in the field. Blessed shall be the fruit of thy body, and the fruit of thy ground, and the fruit of thy cattle, the increase of thy kine, and the flocks of thy sheep. Blessed shall be thy basket and thy store. Blessed shalt thou be when thou comest in, and blessed shalt thou be when thou goest out.

The Lord shall cause thine enemies that rise up against thee to be smitten before thy face: they shall come out against thee one way, and flee before thee seven ways.

The Lord shall command the blessing upon thee in thy storehouses, and in all that thou settest thine hand unto; and he shall bless thee in the land which the Lord thy God giveth thee. The Lord shall establish thee an holy people unto himself, as he hath sworn unto thee, if thou shalt keep the commandments of the Lord thy God, and walk in his ways. And all people of the earth shall see that thou art called by the name of the Lord; and they shall be afraid of thee.

And the Lord shall make thee plenteous in goods, in the fruit of thy body, and in the fruit of thy cattle, and in the fruit of thy ground, in the land which the Lord sware unto thy fathers to give thee. The Lord shall open unto thee his good treasure, the heaven to give the rain unto thy land in his season, and to bless all the work of thine hand: and thou shalt lend unto many nations, and thou shalt not borrow.

And the Lord shall make thee the head, and not the tail; and thou shalt be above only, and thou shalt not be beneath; if that thou hearken unto the commandments of the Lord thy God, which I command thee this day, to observe and to do them: . . .[42]

Jesus confirmed to the disciples that God still desired the prosperity of His children in this life. The new covenant is greater than the old covenant. The new covenant puts the power to keep the law of God inside us. Jesus was made sanctification to us. Because He lives, we live also. Sanctification is no longer an outward performance, but an inner abiding.

When Christ is our life, our outward circumstances mean nothing. Like Paul we can say, "I know both how to be abased, and I know how to abound: every where and in all things I am instructed both to be full and to be hungry, both to abound and to suffer need. I can do all things though Christ which strengtheneth me."[43]

The Kingdom economy is immune to global ups and downs. Paul believed in the Kingdom economy: "But my God shall supply all your need according to his riches in glory by Christ Jesus."[44]

He abounded from every abasement, as his God met his needs according to His riches in glory. God is our source. Jesus came to give us the keys to God's riches, by exchanging His riches for our poverty.

> For ye know the grace of our Lord Jesus Christ, that, though he was rich, yet for your sakes he became poor, that ye through his poverty might be rich.[45]

> And God is able to make all grace abound toward you; that ye, always having all sufficiency in all things, may abound to every good work: . . .[46]

We always have all sufficiency in *all* things. This is dominion living, Kingdom lifestyle. God has given us a down payment big enough to give us joy unspeakable and full of glory.[47] It is enough to meet all our present need according to his riches in glory. It is like Joseph's coat of many colors:[48] it stirs up jealousy and persecution. Joseph was a dreamer of dreams. He expected great things from God, and he got them.

This world was created to be ruled by spiritual, Godlike men. It was created for the blessing of the sons of

God. It yielded its abundance when man was in communion with God, but carnality cursed the earth.

The second Adam brought back the keys to earth's abundance, God's riches in glory. He made it possible again for children of God always to have all sufficiency in *all* things in Him. He removed the curse of the law,[49] the veil that kept man from appropriating all that God has.

There is no more condemnation to them that are in Christ Jesus.[50] All the blessings of heaven are ours in Christ Jesus.[51] When Jesus rose again, He raised us together with Him.[52] When He was glorified and seated at the right hand of God, we were glorified and seated with Him.

Chapter 14

Exalted by God's Love

The Greek word *agape* signifies an absolutely distinct love that is unattainable by humans. It is God's all-consuming love. God Himself is love—infinite, unfathomable, and eternal. The object of that love is you.

Jesus was the perfect expression of God's love for His people. His death on Calvary was the ultimate communication of the Father's heart, which cries out, "I have loved thee with an everlasting love: therefore with lovingkindness have I drawn thee."[1] Jesus embodies the Father's message: "I love you."

The love of God drew us to Christ. The love of God convicted us. The love of God saved us. The love of God sanctifies us. The love of God sustains us. The love of God provides for us. The love of God glorifies us.

Experiencing the *agape* love of God lifts us up from the pit of self-pity and conforms us to the image of Jesus. When we realize how much He loves us, He draws us out of the devastating effects of besetting sin.

The good news of the New Testament is how much God loves us, in spite of ourselves. He sees us complete in Jesus. God has provided the blood of Jesus to wash away our sins, and the Holy Spirit to empower us.

Only in Christ can we realize our eternal potentiality and identity:

- We are complete in Christ. [2]

- We can do all things through Christ.[3]

- We are more than conquerors through Christ.[4]

- Our sufficiency is in Christ.[5]

- We are hidden in Christ.[6]

- We abide in Christ.[7]

- Christ is the express image of the Father's love,[8] and, as we behold the Son, we are daily being perfected into His image.[9]

When we abide in Christ, we abide in His love. The unconditional love of God exalts its object. He gave us the highest honor by making us kings and priests unto Him.

God imparts His glory to the object of His love: His people. We are the temple of His glory. In ourselves, we have no glory. Rather, we have the manifested glory of His abiding presence, through Christ in us. "And the glory which thou gavest me I have given them; that they may be one, even as we are one."[10]

On the cross, Jesus transferred His God-given glory to us. Calvary testifies throughout the ages of how the love of God purchased us to be the dwelling place of that glory. It cost Jesus His own life to obtain our exaltation to glory. "Greater love has no one than this, that a man lay down his life for his friends."[11]

As we have been made one with Christ in His death and resurrection, we are now joint heirs[12] of the glory He had before the foundation of the world. He made us accepted in the beloved.[13] The revelation of the abiding, perfect love of God casts out fear of rejection.[14] Experiencing that love strengthens our faith and gives us full blessed assurance of our salvation.

The joy of knowing God's perfect love delivers us from evil desires, evil tempers, evil thoughts, evil words, and evil works. That revelation will circumcise our hearts and purge us from all sin. The heart is tormented by the beggarly elements[15] of the law, because they cannot set us free from besetting sin. Only the experience of God's love can change our sin nature.

The love of God imparted into our hearts by the Holy Spirit liberates us from me-centeredness. It is only then that the Holy Spirit assures our spirits that we are His, accepted in the beloved. Because we are sons of God, He has given us the spirit of adoption.[16]

The more we know the Lord, the greater is our desire to comprehend, with all the saints, how broad and long and deep and high is the immeasurable love of Jesus Christ, which surpasses all knowledge.[17]

God's love is addictive. The more we appropriate, the more we crave it. We do not quit looking at Jesus because something beautiful and wonderful happened yesterday.

Instead, we press on toward the mark of His high calling, forgetting the things that lie behind.[18]

Those who are coming into personal revelation of the love of God are not found making big claims about themselves, their ministry, or their spirituality. They do not need to make claims for the place where God's grace is bringing them. They are humbled by just a glimpse of the smallest element of their glorious inheritance in Christ.

The infusion of God's love floods their souls like a tidal wave sweeping upon a dry land of self-centeredness. Ambitions fade into insignificance before the increasing brightness of Jesus' glory in His obedient children. On this side of eternity, it is the greatest encounter a man can ever have. Our God is love—abiding, eternal, and intimate.

Our expectation in God is limited to our revelation of His love. If we expect blessings because of what we are, or what we have done, we will miss out. Instead, we must expect everything on the basis of what He is, and what He has done for us. Realizing His love removes all limits to what we can expect. Our faith is quickened when we know that He loves us and delights to bless us abundantly, in spite of ourselves.

James tells us to expect only blessings from our loving Father, because there is no evil in Him. "Every good gift and every perfect gift is from above, and cometh down from the Father of lights, with whom is no variableness, neither shadow of turning."[19]

At Home in the Father's House

The Trinity is love: the Father is love; Jesus is love; The Holy Spirit is love. Only through the illumination of the Holy Spirit can one see that God is absolutely and totally love. No good thing will He withhold from His children.[20] God unilaterally and sovereignly chose you and redeemed you, through the eternal blood of Jesus, to show you His love.

God loves you as you are, where you are. The love of God will transform you. The love of God will preserve you. The love of God will bless you. The love of God will prosper you. The love of God will guide you.

God adopts the rejects and outcasts like you and me into His family. The love of God heals our hurts, when we let God have His way. The love of God comforts us, fills us with joy unspeakable,[21] exalts us, and empowers us. We must allow the love of God to penetrate and permeate our whole being, by simply letting go of all false confidences in the flesh.

On the other hand, the pragmatic, moral, rational approach to life causes spiritual malfunction, because God chose us to be led from above. These humanistic ways by which man seeks meaning and purpose in life lead to disillusionment.

God's solution to man's dilemma is unconditional *agape.* Like the prodigal son,[22] we all wander away when we do not know the heart of the Father. Most Christians live in spiritual pig pens, hurting and isolated. Homecoming is when we stop trying and start trusting.

The Father has not called us to be servants but to be sons. "that we might receive the adoption of sons."[23]

Love is relational and not functional. The revelation of God's love creates an atmosphere of at-homeness in His house. David experienced this sweet communion with God and celebrated his own welcome-home parties whenever he had wandered from trust in the Father. David declares—

> Thou preparest a table before me in the presence of mine enemies: thou anointest my head with oil; my cup runneth over. Surely goodness and mercy shall follow me all the days of my life: and I will dwell in the house of the Lord for ever.[24]

You can never experience spiritual at-homeness with God until you have revelation of the Father's love. The issue is not how much we love God, but how much He loves us. It is not what we have done, but what He has done. He has done it all for us. The extent of that revelation determines the quality of our Kingdom life.

When we are preoccupied with our own performance, it stifles our growth. The servant mentality creates in us a sense of inadequacy and a feeling of strangeness in the Father's house. Though we know better, we are not doing better in our walk. We lack consistency. We feel disqualified by the state of our spiritual lives, and only when we turn our eyes upon Jesus do we walk in victory and joy.

Therefore, every believer must focus again on Jesus, Who is the center of salvation, justification, and sanctification. The dynamic, transforming power is released when we see the love of God for us. That love liberates us from the legalism of will-religion. To know Him in depth and to manifest Him fully in our lives is the goal of every child of God who has experienced His unconditional love.

The carnal mind cannot comprehend the unfathomable love of God toward us. As the veil is drawn back, and we behold the Father's love in the person of Jesus Christ, the limitations imposed by time, the world, and our old nature are removed. The love of God lifts us to realms of the Spirit that are unknown to the natural man.

In Jesus, God has imparted Himself to perform through us and to bear fruit. When we take our eyes away from ourselves and others, and we fix them upon Jesus, the love of God is immediately shed abroad upon our hearts by the Holy Spirit.[25] This is the power that transforms us from within. All fruit is produced in intimacy, which comes only from being at home with God.

Perfected by God's Love

The Father sees us in Christ. This is a glorious mystery, achieved on the cross. It answers Jesus' prayer that we would enter union with Him. "I in them, and thou in me, that they may be made perfect in one; and that the world may know that thou hast sent me, and hast loved them, as thou hast loved me."[26]

Beloved, no matter what man says, there is a high calling upon your life. God has chosen you. Desire only to be in the perfect will of God, glorified and exalted in

Christ. Let faith spring up within you for greater things than you ever dared to believe. Don't allow yourself to be bound by your circumstances, because the infinite love of God will lift you beyond them. He has called you like Moses to blaze a new trail.[27]

God promised that the latter house will be greater than the former.[28] You are God's "latter house" destined for greater glory. He wants men who will move upon this world with the supernatural, showing forth His glory. He provided for you in Christ to join in bringing about His plan for the ages. You will become unconquerable, as you realize God's unconditional love. Though the enemy rages against you, he will not prevail.

Nay, in all these things we are more than conquerors through him that loved us. For I am persuaded, that neither death, nor life, nor angels, nor principalities, nor powers, nor things present, nor things to come, Nor height, nor depth, nor any other creature, shall be able to separate us from the love of God, which is in Christ Jesus our Lord.[29]

Chapter 15

Unified by God's Love

God's plan is for Jesus to have a body of believers through which He can express Himself to the world. Emptied of self and filled with His love, these people are bound together under His lordship, walking in loving fellowship and revealing Him to their generation.

> Herein is my Father glorified, that ye bear much fruit; so shall ye be my disciples. As the Father hath loved me, so have I loved you: continue ye in my love. If ye keep my commandments, ye shall abide in my love; even as I have kept my Father's commandments, and abide in his love.

> These things have I spoken unto you, that my joy might remain in you, and that your joy might be full. This is my commandment, That ye love one another, as I have loved you.[1]

> And the glory which thou gavest me I have given them; that they may be one, even as we are one.[2]

> A new commandment I give unto you, That ye love one another; as I have loved you, that ye also love one another. By this shall all men know that ye are my disciples, if ye have love one to another.[3]

The sign to the world of our sonship is our love for each other. This is how the world is going to know we are His disciples.

> We know that we have passed from death unto life, because we love the brethren. He that loveth not his brother abideth in death. Whosoever hateth his brother is a murderer: and ye know that no murderer hath eternal life abiding in him. Hereby perceive we the love of God, because he laid down his life for us: and we ought to lay down our lives for the brethren.[4]

We love Him because He first loved us.[5] We freely give of ourselves, because we freely received His abiding love.[6] By the Spirit, the saints are sensitized to the needs of others, and they are channels of God's unconditional love.

Christ-in-us binds us together in sweet fellowship and one accord. The elect of God are called out to pioneer a new way, in which giving is living. Love is commitment. Love is loyal, love is faithful, love is involvement, and love is caring.

God wants His children to walk in the light. Our love for each other is a testimony that we must be of God, because flesh cannot love unconditionally.

> Beloved, let us love one another: for love is of God; and every one that loveth is born of God, and knoweth God. He that loveth not knoweth not God; for God is love.

In this was manifested the love of God toward us, because that God sent his only begotten Son into the world, that we might live through him. Herein is love, not that we loved God, but that he loved us, and sent his Son to be the propitiation for our sins.

Beloved, if God so loved us, we ought also to love one another. No man hath seen God at any time. If we love one another, God dwelleth in us, and his love is perfected in us.[7]

The general run of church people have no love or compassion for others, because they have not received the revelation of God's unconditional love. They are still struggling with emotional and spiritual dysfunction. They are hurting and tormented by the shame of their youth. Former things have not passed away in their minds. The old man is still in control.

Self-centeredness indicates lives that have not been yielded to God. Like Israel of old, they are out of Egypt, but Egypt is still in them. They are double-minded and lukewarm. Their vessels are still full of self, and the Lord cannot pour new wine into them.

God is calling His elect out of the world unto Himself. These are great days of revival. Praise God, He is not finished with the Church. She is going to come into perfection of love, right here on earth, and be without spot or wrinkle in these final days.[8] The saints of the end-time Church will exercise dominion over every demon and show forth marvelous works of God, because they will walk in love. Among them there will be no great men, but a great Jesus.

The glory of God on earth is His people walking in unity and love for each other, speaking the same things and having the same mind—the mind of Christ. The world has yet to know by our love for each other that we are His disciples. Only as we turn our eyes away from ourselves and fix them upon Jesus can we see eye-to-eye with each other.

We cannot love one another until we let go of our old human ideas of earning merit with God, because our critical spirit keeps us apart. However, the revelation of His love sets us free from a holier-than-thou spirit of self-centeredness.

As we recognize that Jesus gave Himself for us, we saints need to appropriate His love to enable us to lay down our lives for each other. We learn that we lose nothing by giving. The love of God begets love in us for the brethren. We are made one in Christ.

The glory of sonship is showing the nature of the Father through our personality. In Christ, we bear the Father's image:

- God loves through us.

- God reaches out through us.

- God gives through us.

- God comforts the hurting through us.

- God feeds the hungry through us.

- God encourages the discouraged through us.

- God speaks to His children through us.

- God strengthens the weak through us.

- God builds His people through us.

As the body of Christ, we are the temple of the Holy Spirit, the place where the glory of God abides. God is building us into an organism, not a dead organization. The DNA of the organism is Jesus, the giver of life.

The new creation is a many-member body, with Jesus as the head. Each member shares the glory of the head in a unique way, having its own purpose and function. Through love for one another, the parts come together to display God's glory in Christ:

> From whom the whole body fitly joined together and compacted by that which every joint supplieth, according to the effectual working in the measure of every part, maketh increase of the body unto the edifying of itself in love.[9]

Children of God have one Spirit and one Father. We are family. We are one. We seek to know no man after the flesh.[10] There is no more Jew or Gentile in Christ.

The community of believers is called to a high order of unity in Christ. They are to be in one accord, without sectarianism. When an individual church is not operating in the Spirit, it experiences division, the result of carnality. The people cannot be in one accord apart from the Spirit of God, because the fallen nature is individualistic. Though churchianity has a semblance of unity, it is false unity that is based on a common dogma and not on the Spirit.

The old, Adamic nature can participate in an organization, but not in an organism. Because the organization is man-made, it has no life. It is dead, and it can produce only after its own kind. It is pre-occupied with its own identity and not with Christ-in-you identity. It is run and controlled by big men and knows nothing of the bigness of God. Churchianity is man at his own best.

Jesus said, "I will build my church; and the gates of hell shall not prevail against it."[11] We are living stones being built together into the living temple of God.[12] The master builder has prepared the stones to fit together perfectly and to be bound together by His love.

True unity is supernatural and beyond the capability of flesh. But when the love of God is preached, it transforms people into the image of Jesus Christ. Pastors who let Jesus be the head of His church see the mighty results of His grace and power that love releases among believers.

Lives of ordinary people like you and me are being transformed and changed each day from glory to glory, as we walk in the love of God. We are supernaturally joined in Christ. We bear His image and share His glory as a body united by grace.

Jesus came to reveal a new way of living. He came to destroy egotism in our lives. He has made us joint heirs with Himself of the Kingdom life.[13] He has given us the Comforter,[14] so that we can comfort those who are hurting, with the same comfort that we have received. [15]

We have not reached the ultimate in God. We have barely begun to comprehend the love of God in Christ Jesus, and the unsearchable riches of Christ.[16] God wants to enlarge our capacity to receive and to give His love to our generation. Stretch forth your tent curtains and lengthen your cords.[17]

God wants to pour His love into you. You are a vessel,[18] made to contain His infinite love revealed in Christ Jesus. Because there is no limit, the more we hunger and thirst for His love, the greater the manifestation of His grace toward us. As we realize we are vessels and not producers, it frees us to rest in His love. We receive it freely and can in turn freely pour it out upon others, as vessels fit for the Master's use.[19]

God's perfect love casts away fear of being hurt.[20] Jesus is that perfect love manifested through us. As we behold in Him the glory of the Father and see Him face to face as in a mirror, we are changed from one degree of glory to another.[21] We reflect His glory.

Knowing that love prepares us—like the prodigal son—to receive the garment of righteousness, the ring of authority, and the shoes of leisure, as we enter the Father's welcome party. When we know His heart, it is easy to accept His plan for our lives, because His thoughts toward us are for a future filled with hope.[22] When we yield to Him in childlike dependence, the Holy Spirit actualizes that plan. It is not by might nor by power, but by the Spirit of the Lord.[23]

Those who are born of God love God. It is an inborn disposition. It is part of our new nature in Christ. This love of God works effectively through us to the people with whom we come into contact.

As vessels we express what is inside us. The flesh expresses the flesh, and the spirit expresses the spirit. We express the glory of God, which abides in us. The apostle Paul says: "We have this treasure in earthen vessels, that the excellency of the power may be of God, and not of us."[24] We are vessels. Flesh must die, for the glory to shine through. The less of us, the more the glory of the Father expresses through us.

Made New in Christ

The new man is born of God, and not of the will of man. He is exalted in Christ. This is the foundational truth of the New Testament. In Christ, we have a new identity and new station. Can you imagine the effects on this generation, if believers would walk in the revelation of who they are in God, with power and authority? Jesus came to reproduce Himself in us.

The divine grace bestowed upon us is sufficient[25] in every situation, to make us more than conquerors through Him that loved us.[26] The more yielded we are to God, the greater our authority and dominion over the devil.

We are not the light; it is Jesus shining through us who dispels darkness. Because of Him, we do not need to fight the darkness. Instead, it flees before us. Like a lantern filled with the oil of the Holy Spirit, we illuminate our surroundings by radiating the glory of the indwelling Christ.

Where are the people of God? The dysfunction and instability that characterize most Christians today are signs of spiritual famine for the truth that sets free. The message of "Christ in you, and you in Him," has been lost to the body of Christ. Instead, churches preach dualism: law and grace, faith and works.

We are vessels. We are not originators of holiness, happiness, peace, love, kindness, long suffering. These are fruits of the indwelling Holy Spirit. Vessels contain whatever is put in them.

We are the temple of the Holy Spirit. We are not the light. He is the light in us. He is the lover in us. He is the forgiver in us. He is the joy in us. He is the peace in us. He is the holiness in us. He is the overcomer in us. He is the giver in us. He is the obedience in us. He is the witness in us. He is the glory in us.

This is the crux of the issue: do you have God, or does God have you? What you have, you can lose. Praise God, He is holding you. You can stop holding on, and let God hold you. He can keep you from falling. The blessed assurance is that Jesus is yours.

God radiates His glory most through those people that have let go of their confidence in the flesh. At Peniel, God replaced Jacob's natural strength with a contrite and willing heart ready to do His will.[27] David reminds us in Psalms that God is "my glory, and the lifter up of my head."[28] Our beauty is a reflection of the Sun of righteousness.[29] Our strength and boldness come from the Lion of Judah[30] who lives in us. He is in us to will and to do of His good pleasure.[31]

The joy of the Lord is our strength.[32] Spiritual weakness is a result of spiritual malnutrition. We are what we eat: churchianity feeds God's people junk food. God says, "My people are destroyed for lack of knowledge."[33]

Chapter 16

Kept by Grace

Again the fundamental issue is, do we have the Lord, or does the Lord have us? If we have the Lord, we are obligated to keep Him, in case we lose Him. Is it man's responsibility and daily task to keep God? This was the Galatians' bewitchment.[1] This is nothing but the Old Testament will-religion of works. Although it's preached as grace, it is still man at his best.

In this false gospel, which always emphasizes what you can do for God, man is responsible for keeping God. You "find" Christ. You "make Him" Savior. You "make Him" Lord. You "follow" Him. You "serve" Him. You "obey" Him. This so-called evangelical sound doctrine is dualism and not New Testament Christianity. On the contrary, we are saved by grace alone. We are sanctified by grace alone. We are matured by grace alone. We are complete in Christ by grace alone. He does it all!

This is the good news, the glorious Gospel of the Kingdom. He is the one that came to seek and to save us. The Father chose us from the foundation of the world. The Father draws us to Jesus. Unless the Father draws us to Jesus, it is impossible for our depraved flesh to seek after God. Jesus said to His disciples:

Ye have not chosen me, but I have chosen you, and ordained you, that ye should go and bring forth fruit, and that your fruit should remain: that whatsoever ye shall ask of the Father in my name, he may give it you. [2]

It was not a human initiative by the disciples to find and to follow Jesus. God gave them to Jesus to keep them. Jesus said, "I have manifested thy name unto the men which thou gavest me out of the world: thine they were, and thou gavest them me; and they have kept thy word."[3]

In His *agape* love, God has given Jesus to "whosoever" will believe.[4] Grace is a free gift to whosoever will accept. John says, "But as many as received him, to them gave he power to become the sons of God, even to them that believe on his name."[5]

There is no human achievement in this, but only divine providence of grace. Jesus Christ gives us the power to become sons of God.[6] He forgives our iniquity.[7] He gives us new hearts and writes His laws upon them.[8] He abides in us, to bear fruit that will remain.[9]

He is Lord and Savior. *We* do not make Him Lord and Savior. *God* made Him Lord and Savior. He comes into us as Lord and Savior. He is the author and finisher of our faith.[10]

As Savior He is the author and finisher, the sanctifier. Our sufficiency is in God. We are not saved to serve, but we are saved to be served by the Holy Spirit. The fruit is produced by the Holy Spirit that indwells us. We are just earthen vessels saved by grace.

It is always human to want to help God out. The Jews asked Jesus, "What shall we do, that we might work the works of God?"[11] People today are still asking the same question. The church answers by directing them to do the things that serve the organization. With rules and programs, these "kingdom builders" opiate God's people. However, the true gospel of the Kingdom emancipates the people of God from the will-religion of performance.

The Lord tells us what to do. "Jesus answered and said unto them, This is the work of God, *that ye believe on him whom he hath sent.*"[12]

The work of God is that you believe in His unconditional love, bestowed on you in the person of Jesus Christ. Only believe, and you will see the glory of God. All things are possible to those who believe.[13] Faith pleases the Father. The writer of the Hebrews says: "But without faith it is impossible to please him: for he that cometh to God must believe that he is, and that he is a rewarder of them that diligently seek him."[14]

You must believe that He is. He is El Shaddai, the all-sufficient One.[15] He is your righteousness. He is your peace. He is your victory.

John says, "For whatsoever is born of God overcometh the world: and this is the victory that overcometh the world, even our faith."[16] Faith and not works overcomes the world: faith in the faithfulness of Him that called you.

Both Paul and Jude wrote of God's faithfulness to keep us.[17] You cannot keep God. Let God keep you. You cannot have God. Let God have you. You cannot hold on to God. Let God hold on to you.

In all of us, there is a Peter that wants to wash Jesus' feet. Let Him wash *your* feet. We are like the prodigal Son, wanting to come home and prove ourselves to the Father. Sonship is not serving, but being served. We are joint heirs. The Father wants us to have a party. "This is the work of God, that ye believe on Him, whom He hath sent."[18]

The great mistake of the church today is to disconnect salvation and sanctification. The people are taught that salvation is by grace, but sanctification is by will power or human discipline. Consequently, the new believer struggles in the flesh to overcome. The result is people living in denial, suppression, self-righteousness, and misery for Jesus.

The glorious gospel of Christ in you, the hope of glory, frees the whole man —spirit, soul, and body—to serve the Lord with gladness.[19] Believe me, He is able to do exceeding abundantly above what we can ask or think.[20] Christ will preserve you. Christ will sustain you. Christ will protect you from evil. Christ will empower you. Christ will bear fruit through you.

Sanctified by Grace

Sanctification—separation from sin—is a divine and supernatural work from beginning to end. God makes us pure by His grace, when we are in sustained intimacy with Jesus. By dwelling in Christ, we are made perfect.

The Lord wants us to know that we are purified by the *word* and not works, even as He told the disciples, "Now ye are clean through the word which I have spoken unto you."[21]

How many sermons have you heard that declared that you are complete in Jesus? Jesus said, "The truth shall make you free."[22] You do not need will power to overcome sin; you need the truth to set you free from all compromise and carnality. The devil will flee from "it is written." The gospel is the power of God unto salvation,[23] and with it redemption, justification, sanctification and glorification in one package.

God has given us the Holy Spirit to break the power of sin over our lives. The Spirit brings victory over the buffeting circumstances and the dictates of the flesh. Our old man is crucified with Christ. We must reckon him dead!

Daily God extricates us from the snares of Satan and preserves us. Jesus said, "Those that thou gavest me I have kept, and none of them is lost."[24] The promise is for all ages.

The expression of Christian character is not goodness, but godliness and Christlikeness, because if the Spirit of God has you, He transforms you from within, and your life will exhibit Christ. Your character will reveal Him shining through, and not just human life attempting to be godly.

Made Righteous in Christ

What will free you is not preoccupation with your sin or weakness, but preoccupation with Christ in you. "But of him are ye in Christ Jesus, who of God is made unto us wisdom, and righteousness, and sanctification, and redemption."[25]

To be pleasing to God, we must totally surrender self-will and self-effort, because under the power of the flesh our minds are at enmity with God.[26] That is why our own righteousness is like filthy rags in His sight.[27]

The essence of sin is not particularly what we do; instead, sin occurs when we choose to doubt the One that the Father sent to be our righteousness. Because we are united with Christ in His death and have been raised with him, we have dominion over sin.

For whatsoever is born of God overcometh the world: and this is the victory that overcometh the world, even our faith. Who is he that overcometh the world, but he that believeth that Jesus is the Son of God?[28]

We must realize that Christ is the strength and power that reside inside us. If we fail to partake of His fullness and the promised enabling grace, we are defeated. Let it be clear to every child of God that Jesus is indeed our only holiness. He told us that "without me, you can do nothing."[29]

Jesus triumphed over Satan, hell, and all the principalities and powers of evil for us. Because He rose again and lives, we can live also. He vanquished the enemy for us. It is absolutely certain that no devil can hold you or me down. Our God reigns supreme in heaven, on earth, and under the earth. Christ in you is still defeating the devil through your obedience to the word.

However, our natural tendency is to panic when the devil shows up like a roaring lion.[30] We forget that he is just play acting. He is a has-been. He is powerless and useless. He flees from the name of Jesus.

The church urgently needs to return to the Biblical preaching of the gospel and teach people that the only hope of glory is Christ in you and through you.[31]

John said, "Greater is he that is in you than He that is in the world."[32]

Paul said, "I am crucified with Christ: nevertheless I live; yet not I, but Christ liveth in me."[33]

Jesus does not want to be our helper and assist us to be holy. Instead, He wants to *be* our holiness. He does not want to work with us to be holy. He wants to be our holiness. He does not want us to have our own life; He wants to be our life.

The Holy Spirit actualizes the will of God in and through us as we surrender to Him. He authenticates our sonship by bearing fruit through us. We must not mistake it for our fruit. Christ in us is the originator of all our fruit.

Conscious of Christ in You

The message of Christ in you is at the center of the apostles' teaching. God's emphasis is not on our flesh but on the finished work of our redemption by Jesus, and the present work of cleansing by the Holy Spirit. Flesh profiteth nothing.[34] The only characteristic of the sanctified saints is that they are conscious of Christ in them.

Everything Jesus did was designed to accomplish God's desire to dwell in us. Paul confirms this in his first letter to the Corinthians, when he says—

What? know ye not that your body is the temple of the Holy Ghost which is in you, which ye have of God, and ye are not your own? For ye are bought with a price: therefore glorify God in your body, and in your spirit, which are God's.[35]

We are inhabited by God. We are his temples.[36] We must have a new understanding and appreciation of our commonplace life, because God dwells in us and walks with us even in the humdrum. The supernatural becomes natural in us, as we allow Christ to express Himself through us as earthen vessels.

When believers are not taught about Christ in them, the hope of glory, their assurance of salvation is shaky. That is why Christians are falling apart and looking to psychology for answers. These human solutions for spiritual problems crowd out the "Christ in you" message. Inner tension racks the religiously devout because, as the apostle Paul said, "For I know that in me (that is, in my flesh,) dwelleth no good thing: for to will is present with me; but how to perform that which is good I find not." [37]

True devotion emanates from Christ in you. It devours the flesh and sets the spirit free, inflaming the heart after God as you see how much He is devoted to you. He will never leave you nor forsake you.[38] Rejoice! Nothing can separate you from the love of God in Christ Jesus your Lord.[39]

Your understanding of the doctrine of sanctification determines everything. There is no victory apart from experiencing for yourself Christ in you, the hope of glory. You can know what it means to rest in the Lord and to say with Paul, "I live by the faith in the Son of God, who loved me, and gave himself for me."[40] ... "For to me to live is Christ."[41]

The life of Jesus through you must become such a reality that you live and work among men in the same way He did during His earthly ministry. Your labor of love must be characterized by the joy of the Lord who abides in you. The joy-filled believer thinks, talks, and acts like Jesus, because of His indwelling presence.

Christ in you is God's perfect love dwelling in you. Perfect love casts out fear.[42] The real meaning of the abundant life Jesus came to give us is a life filled with joy unspeakable, full of glory.[43] Sanctification is Christ in you, imparting to you the same disposition that ruled His earthly life.

Christ in you enables you to overcome and transfigures all things with His presence. Christ transforms our self-centered ego by crucifying our old man. He gave us new life, and we can see things from God's perspective.

Our picture of God must change. If you think of spirituality as something impossible for you to attain, you have a wrong picture. Jesus came to demonstrate that God is love. He came to redeem you and to make you part of the family.

The bedrock of Christianity is Christ in you, the hope of glory. The abiding ecstasy in our lives is a daily awareness of the presence of the Lord — Emmanuel, God with us.[44] Jesus is getting us home. He is "the way, the truth, and the life."[45]

Separated unto God

Sanctification means being separated unto God. We have been separated by God to walk with Him like Enoch, Elijah, Paul, and Peter. Christ in you will give you a childlike disposition of absolute dependence on God. He wants so much to keep our lives in step with His plan and purposes. We can count on God to come through. We must become more conscious of His presence with us in the conflicts of life.

God wants to free his children from the tyranny of the flesh. John says, "For this purpose the Son of God was manifested, that He might destroy the works of the devil."[46]

Sanctification is not just being free from sin, but being set apart for God. The glorious gospel transcends the Old Testament law that was limited by the flesh. God sent His own Son in the likeness of sinful flesh, and for sin condemned sin in the flesh. He did this so that the righteousness of the law might be fulfilled in us, who walk not after the flesh but after the Spirit.[47]

The key to victory is entering into the secret place of abiding in Christ and the word. We live not by man's principles, but "by every word that proceedeth out of the mouth of God."[48] All the dos and don'ts preached by the church shape human behavior to look Christian, giving a form of godliness without power.[49]

The church is concerned with externalities, but Jesus said, "The kingdom of God is within."[50] The apostle Paul said, "For the kingdom of God is not meat and drink; but righteousness, and peace, and joy in the Holy Ghost."[51] The Kingdom is righteousness. It is peace. It is joy. This is the essence of the Kingdom of God.

The Holy Spirit in us is the life of God that bears the fruit through our obedience. The indwelling Holy Spirit is not an experience apart from the person of the Lord Jesus. It is the Spirit of Christ. His abiding presence is revealed by the appearance of His attributes in us. That presence of the Spirit of Christ alters everything and transforms us from within.

The religious "kingdom builders" preach righteousness or right-doing, which sounds so good to the moral man. The Pharisees preached right-doing. They substituted that for relationship. They washed the outside of vessels and not the inside. Right-doing sermonettes constitute the crux of the problem with the church today. The church is full of people of right-doing, who are not in right-standing with God and have no intimacy with Him.

These people miss winning the battle, because they continue to try rather than trust. Sadly, they cling to natural virtues and morality, instead of accepting by faith what God has done for them. The Pharisees held on to morality and killed Jesus to preserve it.

The leaven of the Pharisees has permeated the body of Christ. Flesh is being modified and adjusted to be moral and good. God's kingdom plan is not to have good people on earth, but to have sons who enjoy intimacy with Him. Jesus came to give us the glory of the Father. "And the glory which thou gavest me I have given them; that they may be one, even as we are one."[52]

God wants us to walk daily in His glory in Christ Jesus. The ultimate manifestation of that glory is when we will see him face to face. For all eternity we will be like him. "Beloved, now are we the sons of God, and it doth not yet appear what we shall be: but we know that, when he shall appear, we shall be like him; for we shall see him as he is."[53]

The church age is nearly over. The religious system, with its ritualism and formalism, has no future in the age to come. But the elect of God—the invisible church of the saints, born again, abiding in Christ, cleansed in the blood of the lamb, without spot or wrinkle—shall be caught up to be with the Lord.

Chapter 17

Made Holy by the Spirit

The law of God is holy. Jesus did not come to remove the law but to fulfill it. Jesus said, "Think not that I am come to destroy the law."[1] The gospel of the Kingdom does not nullify the law of God. Instead, God made a way for us to fulfill His law by giving Christ to be alive in us, removing the guilt and shame caused by our depravity.

> There is therefore now no condemnation to them which are in Christ Jesus, who walk not after the flesh, but after the Spirit. For the law of the Spirit of life in Christ Jesus hath made me free from the law of sin and death.
>
> For what the law could not do, in that it was weak through the flesh, God sending his own Son in the likeness of sinful flesh, and for sin, condemned sin in the flesh: That the righteousness of the law might be fulfilled in us, who walk not after the flesh, but after the Spirit.[2]

The problem has never been the law of God but the weakness of the flesh, which could not fulfill the demands of a Holy God. The glorious gospel of the cross dealt a fatal blow to the flesh. When Christ was crucified, my old man was crucified;[3] when Jesus was buried, I was buried; and when Jesus rose, I rose a new creation. Jesus took away the power of sin to control me. He broke its hold on me and set me free.

Now we can fulfill the law. The law now describes my new man in Christ. "The law of the Spirit of life in Christ Jesus hath made me free from the law of sin and death."[4]

The law is righteous, but it had no power to impart to my depraved flesh to fulfill its holiness demands. Therefore, I could not appropriate the blessings of the law. The Abrahamic blessings were covenantal, and the law was given as a means to appropriate the blessings. The righteousness of the law maintained the blessings.

Righteousness or right standing with God made it possible for man to have access to God. Since man could never fulfill the covenantal demands of God, He provided animal sacrifice to cover man's sins, and ultimately he provided Jesus to atone for them once and for all.

The blood of Jesus can cleanse us from all unrighteousness.[5] The blood of lambs covered sin, but the blood of Jesus removes sin. Then He gives us the Holy Spirit to empower us to live a righteous life. The righteousness of the law is fulfilled in us, who walk not after the flesh but after the Spirit.[6] Jesus did not come to destroy the law; therefore, living by grace is not living *in* sin, but living *above* sin, by the indwelling Holy Spirit.

Christ in us keeps the law. Christ the life-giver and law-giver is now the law-lover in us. He took upon himself the curse of the law and left for you and me the blessings of the law. He fulfilled the covenantal demands for us, so that by faith we can appropriate all the blessings of Abraham in Christ.

Both the physical and the spiritual seed of Abraham can realize the inheritance. God made a covenant with Abraham 430 years before He gave the law on Mt. Sinai. The covenant established a unique, special relationship between God and Abraham. Jesus came to fulfill the Abrahamic covenant. He opened a new and living way for all mankind to come into the commonwealth of Israel, and have access to the God of Abraham, Isaac, and Jacob. He removed the wall of partition, the enmity, and our indictment, and nailed it all to the cross. [7]

The holiness demanded by the law now comes forth in us by the law of life in Christ Jesus. Christ in us loves the law of God. Christ through us fulfills the law of God.

The message of Christ in you—sanctification by grace—is not "Do what you want, and God will forgive you." It is a message of holiness with happiness. It is not a message of excusing your flesh, and accusing God or others for making it too hard. It is a message of taking full responsibility for your actions and confessing as David did: "Wash me thoroughly from mine iniquity, and cleanse me from my sin. For I acknowledge my transgressions: and my sin is ever before me."[8]

God has made provision for our past, present, and future sins through the blood of Jesus. The new man in Christ cannot live in sin, but he can fall. When it happens, John tells us to confess. "If we confess our sins, he is faithful and just to forgive us our sins, and to cleanse us from all unrighteousness."[9]

God hated sin in the Old Testament, He hates sin in the New Testament, and He will hate sin for all eternity. Grace is God's way of removing the power of sin in our lives. Many evangelicals misunderstand the difference between grace and legalism. They think legalism demands too much holiness, while grace tolerates and accommodates violations of the law.

Rather, legalism is doing the law by the flesh, and grace is doing the law through the Spirit. Grace is not making Christianity more livable, more compassionate, more understanding, and more tolerant of compromise. Jesus said, "For verily I say unto you, Till heaven and earth pass, one jot or one tittle shall in no wise pass from the law till all be fulfilled."[10]

Without holiness, no man can see God. The word says, "Be ye holy, for I am holy."[11] There is no lowering of standards in the New Testament. The gospel of cheap grace encourages people to continue to live in compromise, unlike the early church, which did not compromise divine holiness or the law of God.

Paul says, "Put ye on the Lord Jesus Christ, and make not provision for the flesh, to fulfil the lusts thereof."[12] The Old Testament children of Israel made provision for the flesh, because they did not have the Holy Spirit living in them and empowering them to overcome. The New Testament saints have Christ in them to enable them to defeat sin, instead of providing for it. "For the law of the Spirit of life in Christ Jesus hath made me free from the law of sin and death."[13]

The popular statement that "I am a sinner saved by grace" gives a wrong perception to the saints. We are saints saved by grace. We are not sinners living in sin and being forgiven because of Jesus, as if God made it easy on the flesh in the New Testament.

It is human to sin. That is why Jesus crucified the flesh. He doesn't go along with our flesh. He demands absolute holiness, without which no man can see God.

We are saints, set apart to live unto God by grace alone. God by grace provided blood to cleanse us and by grace fills us with His Holy Spirit so we can live in holiness unto Him. And when we turn back from taking our eyes off Jesus, He is just and faithful to forgive us and to cleanse us from all unrighteousness with His blood.[14] The gospel of the Kingdom puts the Kingdom of God inside us.

Living in sin is not Kingdom living. It is not grace living. It is not New Testament lifestyle. It is human lifestyle. It is old-man lifestyle. It is religious lifestyle. The gospel lifestyle is righteousness, peace, and joy in the Holy Ghost.[15] Churchianity teaches us to suppress the old man, while the scriptures clearly tell us to eradicate him.

Paul says, "I am crucified with Christ: nevertheless I live; yet not I, but Christ liveth in me: and the life which I now live in the flesh I live by the faith of the Son of God, who loved me, and gave himself for me."[16]

Reckon your old man dead. The old man tries to come back to control, and the new man counteracts him through the power of the Spirit. Don't invite the old man back. Don't make room for him. "Resist the devil, and he will flee from you."[17]

128

Today's church accommodates the flesh and tries to clean it up. The early church confronted sin head on. They were not afraid to lose people. They didn't compromise. They preached holiness with happiness, but modern holiness preachers bring God's people back to bondage instead.

The fruit of such legalism is a morbid type of holiness, without happiness. The more miserable the person looks, the more they are regarded as holy. It is all constrained-works holiness, without the Spirit. It is all play acting. It lacks power.

The early church had power with God. Holiness produces power. Holiness produces happiness. Holiness produces victory. Holiness produces compassion. Holiness produces boldness. Holiness produces unity. Holiness produces divine order in the family. Holiness produces wholesome relationships.

Churchianity conditions people to live in defeat and compromise. It preaches sermons catering to man's depravity. These affirmations of human weakness sound so spiritual, but they are lies from the pit of hell. You are not weak. You are not a sinner but a saint. You are not bad. You are a new creation in Christ. You are strong in the Lord. You have a new and holy disposition, because you partake of His divine nature. You are an overcomer. You are complete in Christ.

Victorious Through the Truth

The devil is the father of lies,[18] who comes only to steal and to kill. Praise God, Jesus came to give you abundant life.[19] You don't have to accept the degradation of sin. You don't have to obey the dictates of the flesh. Cease from all labor and enter the Father's rest.[20]

Churchianity controls the people of God by the yoke of the law. Christ removes the yoke[21] and sets the captives free.[22] He gives grace upon grace. He gives beauty for ashes, and a garment of praise for the spirit of heaviness.[23]

The gospel of the kingdom is God's good news to the outcasts, yet the world has yet to see a happy and holy people of God living in victory. The good news is not about what you have done for God, but what God has done for you in Christ.

In the forefront of this marvelous gospel stands this affirmation: "God loves you." These are the grandest words in the ears of every person who hears what the Spirit is saying. This is the Rock of Gibraltar upon which we build our faith. Nothing can separate us from the love of God in Christ Jesus.[24] The only limit is our faith and our expectation. "If God be for us who can be against us?"[25]

Failure is caused by focusing on human capacity to please God and to resist the devil, who is intent on hindering God's purposes. Before God established the world, He ordained good works for His New Testament people to do.[26] Therefore, for the church to teach them that sin is a normal Christian experience is to dispossess them of their appointed position in Christ.

Christians are to live by responsive, ever-growing faith in the indwelling Christ. We must capitulate to His total control and be totally filled with His life. As children of God, we must not make occasion for sin. Sin is out of character with our new nature in Christ.

We are crucified to the world, and the world is crucified in us, who live not after the flesh but after the Spirit.[27] It is not our own will power that constrains our flesh from besetting sin. Instead it is the truth that sets us free.[28] The truth leads to sanctification and holiness.

Jesus never told his disciples to sanctify themselves, but he prayed that the Father would sanctify them.[29] Human initiative by itself cannot sanctify the soul.

Justification is our position in Christ, and sanctification is the process by which the Holy Spirit conforms us to the image of Jesus Christ. The Holy Spirit cleans and purifies us to make us holy as He is holy. Sanctification is provided by grace, which we appropriate by faith.

The purpose of our sonship is to please the Father like Jesus. He is delighted in us as we abide in Christ by faith.

How does God sanctify us? Jesus tells us how: "Sanctify them through thy truth; thy word is truth."[30] The truth purifies us. The truth liberates us. The truth transforms us. The truth re-images us into Christlikeness. The truth glorifies us.

What is that emancipating truth? It is specific truth. It is the glorious truth of the Kingdom of God within us,[31] Christ in us the hope of glory.[32]

The letter of the law kills,[33] but the truth that sanctifies is a living and experiential word. It is "it is written" quickened within us by the Spirit.

The sanctifying truth has its origin in God. It is God's spoken word, the bread of life. Jesus said, "Man shall not live by bread alone, but by every word that proceeds from the mouth of God."[34] God is speaking love, peace, and joy into His people. You and I are the object of God's love and power, which can lift us up above disillusionments of life.

Holiness is being wholly occupied by Christ. He is greater than the one that is in the world.[35] He triumphed over hell. He rose again from the dead. He is alive and you are alive in Him. The battle is over! It is done! It is finished! You are doing the done. Christ is your holiness. He is in you to will and to do of his good pleasure.

Have faith in God. All things are possible to them that believe that Jesus has been made unto you wisdom, righteousness, sanctification, redemption, and peace.[36] We receive what we believe. We become what we believe, when we stand upon the word.

The practical application of the truth sets us free to serve God with gladness, because sanctification ultimately means sharing the life of God in Christ. You are the branch. He is the vine. The fruit is the expression of the life of the vine. Abide in the vine and you will bear much fruit, and your fruit will remain.[37] You are set apart to share his image and glory.

Let faith spring up within you for greater things than you ever dared to believe. Have faith: He that began a good work in you will finish it.[38] He is faithful. Put your faith in him.

He is your righteousness, entitling you to come boldly into the Holy of Holies.[39] You have been made accepted in the beloved.[40] As you behold Him, you will be changed from one degree of glory to another.[41] Fix your eyes upon Him. He is the author and finisher of your faith.[42]

You stand at the threshold of a glorious hour in God. I invite you, like the apostle Paul, to be found in Christ having only the righteousness that comes through faith, and moving forward into the future God has planned for you. This is my heart for you. This is my vision. This is my longing:

> Yea doubtless, and I count all things but loss for the excellency of the knowledge of Christ Jesus my Lord: for whom I have suffered the loss of all things, and do count them but dung, that I may win Christ, And be found in him, not having mine own righteousness, which is of the law, but that which is through the faith of Christ, the righteousness which is of God by faith:
>
> That I may know him, and the power of his resurrection, and the fellowship of his sufferings, being made conformable unto his death; If by any means I might attain unto the resurrection of the dead.
>
> Not as though I had already attained, either were already perfect: but I follow after, if that I may apprehend that for which also I am apprehended of Christ Jesus.

Brethren, I count not myself to have apprehended: but this one thing I do, forgetting those things which are behind, and reaching forth unto those things which are before, I press toward the mark for the prize of the high calling of God in Christ Jesus.[43]

Chapter 18

Transformed by Grace

It is impossible to be victorious without understanding the unconditional love of God and His unmerited favor. One has to know deep down that salvation, sanctification, and glorification are by faith alone (*sola fide*), by grace alone (*sola gratia*), and by Christ alone (*sola Christus*). Christ crucified and then risen constitutes the whole gospel. He is the author and finisher of our faith. The gospel is the power of God unto holiness. It is a finished work!

The church's dilemma is that grace preaching has usually produced irresponsibility and indulgence. This is a normal flesh reaction to the grace message. Flesh appreciates it and then proceeds to take advantage of the forgiving grace of God.

On the other hand, the law contains the flesh. Fear of the consequences drives people to suppress or deny the flesh, but never to reach out for a love affair with Jesus.

Grace is not taught but caught. The grace message is a message of holiness living, through the indwelling Holy Spirit. Grace is not an evangelical doctrine. It is an encounter with the living God.

The New Testament message of grace transformed the early church into the image of Jesus Christ. People called them Christians, meaning "Christ-like." The early church had the power of God operating in it.

In the modern version of the grace message, the problem is lack of power. The message of grace without the power of the indwelling Holy Spirit leads to compromise and carnality.

Today's message of grace is cheap gospel, which says, "Do the best you can, and God will forgive the rest." The man-made grace message accommodates besetting sin. Grace as understood in the body of Christ today is loose application of God's holiness standard established by His law.

The difference between the Old Testament and the New Testament is not a lower standard, but believers empowered by the Holy Spirit to fulfill it. The law now describes the New Testament believers' lifestyle. Grace produces holiness with happiness. Grace overcomes sin. Grace liberates!

When the apostles preached grace, they declared that righteousness does not consist of the dead works of the law, but a vital, living relationship with God. What God wanted from His people was relationship and not performance. He made His grace manifest in the person of Jesus Christ.

> And of his fulness have all we received, and grace
> for grace. For the law was given by Moses, but
> grace and truth came by Jesus Christ.[1]

Grace is that God gave us Jesus to become our righteousness. He is our holiness. Grace is Christ in us, the hope of glory. It is not an impartation of special strength to the flesh. Scriptures are clear that it is no longer I that live, but Christ lives in me.[2] I am no longer a producer but a vessel housing Christ. His holiness is now my holiness. His joy is my joy. His peace is my peace. His life is my life. This is grace, amazing grace!

Therefore, we cannot separate regenerating grace from sanctifying grace and glorifying grace. The grace of God is God imparting Himself to me in the person of the Holy Spirit to indwell me. This is the good news of grace. This is a glorious dispensation, the epoch of the Holy Spirit, the age of the new man in Christ. The new creation is made in the likeness of Jesus. It is victorious in Jesus. It is preserved in Christ. It is kept by His power.

Man's good works proceed either from legalism or from the fruit of the Spirit. The meritorious works of the flesh are like filthy rags. The New Testament calls them dead works of the law which cannot justify man in the sight of God.

> But that no man is justified by the law in the sight of God, it is evident: for, The just shall live by faith.[3]

The New Testament saints live by faith, in the abiding presence of the Holy Spirit. The grace message does not substitute for the holiness message of the Old Testament. The law still applies to the saints. The scriptures clearly teach us that without holiness no man can see God. Then how do New Testament saints fulfill the law? Through the Holy Spirit, who lives in them.

God's grace is manifested toward us in three ways: Jesus' dying to save us from the wages of sin, the Holy

Spirit's abiding in us to overcome sin, and Jesus' return to take us to glory.

Therefore, the *saving* grace is "Christ *for* me." He came for me. He died for me. He ascended to the right hand of God for me. He daily makes intercession for me. He is coming back for me. He is for me!

The *sanctifying* grace is "Christ *in* me." Christ in me my holiness. Christ in me my peace. Christ in me my joy. Christ in me my strength. Christ in me my sufficiency. Christ in me my wisdom. Christ in me my happiness. Christ in me my victory. He is in me!

The *reigning* grace is Christ *through* me. Christ through me my fruit. Christ through me my witness. Christ through me my compassion for the lost. Christ through me my character. Christ through me my worship. Christ through me my prayer. Christ through me my ministry.

The apostle Paul says, "For it is God which worketh in you both to will and to do of his good pleasure."[4] He is through you!

In *redeeming* grace, Christ *died as* me. He died as my substitute. He paid my debt. He died that I may not die. He became Son of Man that I might become son of God. He came to earth that I might go to heaven. He came into time, space, and matter that He might take me to eternity. He is my elder brother, my kinsman redeemer.

Sustaining grace is *because He lives, I live also*.[5] I was raised up with Christ.[6] He is the new man in me.[7] He will keep me from falling.[8] He will never leave me nor forsake me.[9] I shall abide in His temple forever.[10]

I do not keep the Lord; He keeps me. My life is hid in God with Christ Jesus.[11] Nothing shall ever pluck me out of His hand.[12] His grace is sufficient for me. [13] Nothing shall separate me from the love of God in Christ Jesus my Lord.[14]

The *glorifying* grace has seated me with Christ in heavenly places.[15] I am a joint heir with Christ of all things.[16] He has given me all things pertaining to life and godliness.[17] We are partakers of the glory of God.[18] Jesus gave us the glory of the Father.

And the glory which thou gavest me I have given them; that they may be one, even as we are one: I in them, and thou in me, that they may be made perfect in one; and that the world may know that thou hast sent me, and hast loved them, as thou hast loved me. [19]

We were chosen to inherit the Kingdom; Jesus said, "It is your Father's good pleasure to give you the kingdom."[20] He has given us beauty for ashes, the garment of praise for the spirit of heaviness.[21] The glory of God is already within us. When He shall appear we shall be like Him,[22] because as He is, so are we. [23] The glory of the Lord is being imparted to us in an ever-increasing measure as we fix our eyes upon Jesus daily.

But we all, with open face beholding as in a glass the glory of the Lord, are changed into the same image from glory to glory, even as by the Spirit of the Lord.[24]

Transformed by the Comforter

Jesus came to demonstrate the love of God and to impart God's love to us. However, our human minds cannot fully comprehend the infinite love of God. Only the Holy Spirit can deepen our insight into the mystery of Christ in us, the hope of glory.[25]

Through the indwelling and abiding presence of the Holy Spirit, God executes His glorious plan of blessing for our lives. His purpose through the ages has been to transform us into vessels of His glory.

> Blessed be the God and Father of our Lord Jesus Christ, who hath blessed us with all spiritual blessings in heavenly places in Christ:
>
> According as he hath chosen us in him before the foundation of the world, that we should be holy and without blame before him in love:
>
> Having predestinated us unto the adoption of children by Jesus Christ to himself, according to the good pleasure of his will, To the praise of the glory of his grace, wherein he hath made us accepted in the beloved.[26]

When we experience the infinite love of God, the whole panorama of divine revelation throughout the scriptures acquires a tremendous personal significance. We were blind until the Holy Spirit opened our eyes to see that love in the cross of Jesus Christ. Now the Holy Spirit changes our perspective, disclosing the inexhaustible love, the unspeakable joy, and the inconceivable abundance God has for us.

The work of the Holy Spirit is to keep the cross and its surpassing love at the center of our lives. Jesus said:

> But when the Comforter is come, whom I will send unto you from the Father, even the Spirit of truth, which proceedeth from the Father, he shall testify of me:[27]

In contrast, the natural man is oriented towards the things of this world. The carnal mind cannot appreciate the things of the Spirit. Without the enabling of the Holy Spirit, born-again, Bible-believing, God-loving, church-going saints are impotent to resist the flesh. That is why Jesus came: to give us dynamic power for living a holy life. He likened each of us to branches that receive life from the vine.

> I am the vine, ye are the branches: He that abideth in me, and I in him, the same bringeth forth much fruit: for without me ye can do nothing.[28]

The tragedy is that the church appeals to the flesh to be good, and as a result the church is full of "good people." God is looking for godliness, not goodliness.

The Christians in Galatia fell back under this spell of legalism, and it robbed them of vitality and victory. Paul's letter to them is a warning as well to the church today:

> O foolish Galatians, who hath bewitched you, that ye should not obey the truth, before whose eyes

Jesus Christ hath been evidently set forth, crucified among you?

This only would I learn of you, Received ye the Spirit by the works of the law, or by the hearing of faith? Are ye so foolish? having begun in the Spirit, are ye now made perfect by the flesh?[29]

All human effort is inadequate to accomplish the will of God, because flesh is chiefly dispositioned towards evil. Paul says, "For I know that in me (that is, in my flesh,) dwelleth no good thing."[30]

Only the indwelling Holy Spirit can wipe out the effects of the sin that assails us. Our victorious testimony is clearly the work of the Holy Spirit radiating through us. It is only the Spirit that leads us into absolute obedience of faith.

As God embraces us and lifts us up in loving kindness, He carries out His eternal purposes with our lives. He transforms us by His love, and He empowers us by the person of the Comforter or Paraclete—the Holy Spirit.

We must always bear in mind that sanctification was part of the redemption package. That is how we avoid the temptation of taking ourselves too seriously, trying to sanctify ourselves by will-power obedience. Instead, we can rely totally on the Holy Spirit, who spurs us to joyous confidence of faith and practical victorious living.

The Holy Spirit establishes the sovereignty of God and brings the fulfillment in our lives of "Thy will be done on earth as it is in heaven." We are an organism of the Kingdom of God on earth. We are its ambassadors, and its authority stands behind us.

Through the indwelling Holy Spirit, we saints are in a vital living relationship to Christ, as His body. The Holy Spirit is the source of that union. Our victory is the manifestation of Christ in us.

Now thanks be unto God, which always causeth us to triumph in Christ, and maketh manifest the savour of his knowledge by us in every place.[31]

Our victory is always to the same degree that we surrender to the power that raised Christ from the dead. The Holy Spirit desires to possess our whole person— spirit, soul, and body—as the temple of God. He wants to fill us with His glory. Paul says:

What? know ye not that your body is the temple of the Holy Ghost which is in you, which ye have of God, and ye are not your own? For ye are bought with a price: therefore glorify God in your body, and in your spirit, which are God's.[32]

The glorious power we possess as believers lies in the fact that we are merely containers to house the Holy Spirit. In essence, our lives just reflect the glory of the risen Christ. We have nothing of ourselves. Therefore, our goal is to allow Jesus complete lordship.We must make the course of our lives an unfolding tapestry of God's will, ordained before the foundation of the world.

For by grace are ye saved through faith; and that not of yourselves: it is the gift of God: Not of works, lest any man should boast. For we are his

workmanship, created in Christ Jesus unto good
works, which God hath before ordained that we
should walk in them.[33]

As the object of divine workmanship, our lives
manifest the will of God as much as we yield ourselves to
Him in joyous service, bearing the fruits of the Spirit as
obedient sons.

Chapter 19

You Deserve the Best

You are bigger than you think you are. You have more than you realize, because there is untapped potential in you. Inside you is a spiritual dynamo, ready to be put into operation.

You can rise above your circumstances to new heights of glory. New horizons are waiting for your exploration. Your problems are really opportunities and stepping stones to a higher plane of existence.

There is a dimension of existence where life is a festival of celebration. Nothing can stop you from becoming one of the happiest people on earth. You were created to enjoy life to the fullest.

Are you ready to appropriate your inheritance? You must begin where you are. To do that, you need to know why you are where you are, and how you got there. It is because of your inheritance as a human being.

Your roots as a human are tied to the fate of the first man, Adam. God had a dream from ages past. He created the heavens and the earth to accomplish it. Man was the dream! God worked for five days to prepare a beautiful universe and, finally, the Garden of Eden. He made all these arrangements for man to enjoy. On the sixth day, when everything stood ready, He made Adam and Eve.

They were the crown of creation. God gave man and woman an elite status: of all the creatures on earth, He made them alone to be like Himself.

And God said, Let us make man in our image, after our likeness: and let them have dominion over the fish of the sea, and over the fowl of the air, and over the cattle, and over all the earth, and over every creeping thing that creepeth upon the earth.[1]

Man is God's best, created for the best. He made man for royalty, to share dominion on earth with Him. Upon man God bestowed the unique capacity to fellowship with Him and to enjoy eternity with Him. Space, time, and matter were subject to man, whom God designed to outlive this present earthly system.

God is a God of order. Divine order flows out of His infinite love. At the time He created man, He had made order out of the cosmic disorder and then established the Garden of Eden for man's perpetual celebration. That order was His divine guarantee for the ultimate best for man.

The devil, the author of confusion, fear, and death, hated to see man enjoy life in the presence of God. He deceived man and robbed him of his elite status.

The tragedy of the Fall was the end of the celebration God intended for man. Joy was replaced with sorrow. Life, with death. Blessing, with curse. Divine order, with

Babel. Love, with hate. Music, with mourning. Glory, with groaning.

The unregenerate man was displaced and dispositioned in God's economy of blessings. He was disinherited and deprived. The devil totally dispossessed man; apart from Jesus, man had nothing and was nothing.

Immediately after the Fall, man began struggling to recreate the Garden of Eden, but to no avail. Man was, and still is, under the lie that he can attain joy apart from God. That spiritual vacuum in man created an unquenchable quest for fulfillment.

God did not give up His dream for man. He still wants the best for man. God is rebuilding that dream in the person of His Son Jesus. The good news of the Gospel is that man can be happy again, in God; he can regain the place of royalty that he lost.

On the face of the earth there is a community that is born again from above. God's dream is being realized and fulfilled by men from every walk of life. These are the happiest people on the earth. Jesus bought them with his own blood, making it possible again for them to be called sons of God.

> To redeem them that were under the law, that we might receive the adoption of sons. And because ye are sons, God hath sent forth the Spirit of his Son into your hearts, crying Abba, Father.[2]

The redeemed share in the joy of sonship. David called it "the joy of salvation" in Psalm 51. Adam and Eve before the Fall were the happiest people on earth, because of the presence of God. Once again, the redeemed can abide in the Lord.

Abide in me, and I in you. As the branch cannot bear fruit of itself, except it abide in the vine; no more can ye, except ye abide in me.[3]

Happiness is abiding in the presence of the Eternal One. Man's fullest potential and his unfathomable joy come from staying in God's presence. This is the realm that Jesus unlocked for the believer.

Thou wilt shew me the path of life: in thy presence is fulness of joy; at thy right hand there are pleasures for evermore.[4]

There is no such thing as being miserable for Jesus. Jesus was the last sacrifice. He paid the full price. Miserable Christians are not miserable because they are sacrificing for Jesus; they are miserable because they do not abide in the presence of the Lord. They have little pleasure in life, because they do not know the Lord's right hand, where there are pleasures forevermore.

Living in the secret place of the Most High is living in divine security.[5] It is a place of victory. This is not a futuristic, by-and-by, someday-in-heaven thing. This is something that you can enter into today. The psalmist David knew that place. You also can know that place of quiet rest.

Although once you sat in the rubble of torn clothes and ashes, you no longer hear the voice of the devil that condemns you to die beneath the law of sin and death.

Your savior has defeated death, and you have been set free by the Spirit of liberty of life in Christ Jesus.

Hallelujah! You can rise out of your circumstances, dust yourself off, remove the tattered clothing, and cast away the spirit of heaviness. You can stand before your Lord to receive the linen garment of righteousness and have the oil of gladness poured upon your head. You no longer look back to that ash heap, but you look at where you are now in Christ and where you are going.

> Looking unto Jesus the author and finisher of our faith; who for the joy that was set before him endured the cross, despising the shame, and is set down at the right hand of the throne of God.[6]

> I press toward the mark for the prize of the high calling of God in Christ Jesus.[7]

The earth was cursed because of sin, but Jesus took the punishment upon Himself. He removed from us the curse and its consequences.

> Christ hath redeemed us from the curse of the law, being made a curse for us: for it is written, Cursed is every one that hangeth on a tree.[8]

We are redeemed. We are free from the curse. Instead of being cursed, we are blessed!

Through faith, the blessings of Abraham are ours, and we are inheritors of the promises. We are sealed in by a covenant that stands against any impediment to our receiving God's love.

For I am persuaded, that neither death, nor life,
nor angels, nor principalities, nor powers, nor
things present, nor things to come, nor height, nor
depth, nor any other creature, shall be able to
separate us from the love of God, which is in
Christ Jesus our Lord.[9]

Celebrate the Best!

The most exciting result of being a triumphant
believer is the natural expression of thanksgiving, praise,
and worship. When the Apostle John was caught up into
heaven, he saw and heard a vast congregation in the
celebration of praise to Jesus Christ.

And I beheld, and I heard the voice of many
angels round about the throne and the beasts and
the elders: And the number of them was ten
thousand times ten thousand, and thousands of
thousands;

Saying with a loud voice, Worthy is the Lamb that
was slain to receive power, and riches, and
wisdom, and strength, and honor, and glory, and
blessing.[10]

Praise is the very breath of heaven and the language of
the whole family of God. True praise is based upon God's
character revealed in the word.

Praise brings the manifestation of victory. Faith is
praise. It is not waiting in a vacuum for God to show
forth the victory. Praise is the substance of faith.
Abraham's faith was revealed by praise.

He staggered not at the promise of God through unbelief; but was strong in faith, giving glory to God;

And being fully persuaded that, what he had promised, he was able also to perform.

And therefore it was imputed to him for righteousness.[11]

The expression of his reliance on God's promise was praise. He gave God the glory by faith. He based his faith upon God's faithfulness. This is the sacrifice of praise offered before the victory is seen.

By him therefore let us offer the sacrifice of praise to God continually, that is, the fruit of our lips giving thanks to his name.[12]

In David's long life of military and spiritual conflict, he walked in victory because he had learned that the secret of victory is praise. The people of God need to operate in the same dimension in which David flowed. He was an overcomer because of his celebration of praise.

I will bless the Lord at all times: his praise shall continually be in my mouth.[13]

A triumphant believer is one continually caught up in the celebration of praise.

Giving thanks to the Father, who has qualified us to share in the inheritance of the saints in light.[14]

In the life of a believer, praise has nothing to do with circumstances. It flows out of what God has already done in Jesus for us.

Thanks be unto God for his unspeakable gift.[15]

The festivity of praise is not something one has to wait to *feel* before expressing. It is an act of the will, based upon faith in God's word.

Rooted and built up in him, and stablished in the faith, as ye have been taught, abounding therein with thanksgiving.[16]

Thanksgiving is part of praise. Praise is thanksgiving, but it is based upon faith and not fact. Praise and thanksgiving are responses to the redemptive work of Christ.

In everything give thanks: for this is the will of God in Christ Jesus concerning you.[17]

There is also thanksgiving based upon accomplished fact. God has just done something, and you thank Him for it.

And immediately he received his sight, and followed him, glorifying God: and all the people, when they saw it, gave praise unto God.[18]

Thanksgiving for victory that is already achieved or revealed does not take faith. It flows out of gratitude, while praise precedes manifestation.

152

The celebration of praise should be a believer's daily experience of joy.

> Rejoice in the Lord alway: and again I say, Rejoice.[19]

God has designed the whole cosmic order to bless you. He has strategically positioned you for blessings in Christ.

> And we know that all things work together for good to them that love God, to them who are the called according to his purpose.[20]

You are blessed when you wake up in the morning. You are blessed as you lie down. You are blessed as you go in and out.[21] You are a **winner** in God. You are blessed all around and all year round, because your heart is at the right place.

You Are the Best

Once one knows who he is "in Christ," it is time to step out in faith and put that knowledge into practice. Normal Christian living is daily victorious Christian living. A born-again, Spirit-filled, word-talking believer is on the winning side.

> For whatsoever is born of God overcometh the world: and this is the victory that overcometh the world, even our faith. Who is he that overcometh the world, but he that believeth that Jesus is the Son of God? [22]

Faith is the victory that overcomes the world: faith in the word of God, faith in the faithfulness of God, faith in the finished work of redemption, faith in the unconditional love of God, faith in the name of Jesus— the name above all names.

Victory is not a change in circumstances. Victory is not feeling good about the situation. Victory is not victory, unless it is in faith. Faith is victory!

Victory is a walk: it is not a work. You don't work through situations, you walk through them. Faith is a walk.

For we walk by faith, not by sight.[23]

Walking by feelings is walking by sight. Watching for the change in the situation is walking by sight. But walking by faith is standing on God's promises.

It is thinking the word.

It is talking the word.

It is acting the word.

It is living out the word.   .

This is *positional* victory. There can never be *practical* victory without positional victory. Positional victory was accomplished two thousand years ago. When Jesus died on the cross, he dispossessed the devil. Legally, He gave you total victory by reinstating you to man's original position of majesty and power above

Satan. He put Satan under your feet, forever. This victory is eternal victory!

The victory has been won in the Spirit. The war is over. The devil was the loser. You cannot defeat any enemy that has already been defeated.

These things I have spoken unto you, that in me ye might have peace. In the world ye shall have tribulation: but be of good cheer; I have overcome the world.[24]

Jesus overcame the world for you, so that you could enter into that victory. To enter into strife and struggle is to admit that the enemy has not been defeated. That is exactly what Satan wants us to believe. However, God has enabled us to deal with him in a way different from fleshly conflict.[25]

Spiritual warfare is fought by putting on the whole armor of God. Before we put on His armor, we must cast off any filthy rags of self-righteousness and stand naked before our God to be cleansed by confessing our sins and receiving His forgiveness.

Then and only then may we prepare to put on God's armor. Next, we must release and throw off whatever yoke of personal cares, concerns, and worries are loading us down. In exchange, we may slip onto our shoulders the joyful service to which He has called us.

Come unto me, all ye that labour and are heavy laden, and I will give you rest. Take my yoke upon you, and learn of me; for I am meek and lowly in heart: and ye shall find rest unto your souls. For my yoke is easy, and my burden is light.[26]

Now we may put on our Father's armor: First the linen garment of righteousness[27] as our breastplate, a covering of truth buckled at our waists, sandals of readiness to carry the good news of peace, the shield of faith held before us, the helmet of salvation on our heads, and the sword of the spirit in our hands. [28]

If we try and fight the devil with our own armor or without the power of the Holy Spirit, we risk the same defeat as the sons of Sceva experienced.[29] Therefore, it is vital that we put on the whole armor of God, daily.

For we wrestle not against flesh and blood, but against principalities, against powers, against the rulers of the darkness of this world, against spiritual wickedness in high places.[30]

For the weapons of our warfare are not carnal, but mighty through God to the pulling down of strong holds.[31]

Once you put on the whole armor of God, you start cheering up, as you watch the Lord fight for you.

For the Lord your God is he that goeth with you, to fight for you against your enemies, to save you. [32]

Positional victory is knowing that the battle is not yours. Once you come to terms with that, you cease striving and enter into God's rest.

There remaineth therefore a rest to the people of God. For he that is entered into his rest, he also hath ceased from his own works, as God did from his.[33]

Positional victory is rest. The overwhelming sense of peace and joy in the midst of chaos is born out of a knowledge that victory is assured.

Now thanks be unto God, which always causeth us to triumph in Christ, and maketh manifest the savour of his knowledge by us in every place.[34]

He always leads us in triumph. We never lead ourselves to victory, no matter how we try. Victory is never earned. It is never won. It is given.

Jesus always leads his children to greater victory. It is never from defeat to victory, because positionally a believer is always in victory, although in a practical sense he may go through some rough times. Positional victory leads to practical victory through faith.

There are no impossibilities with faith.

But Jesus beheld them, and said unto them, With man this is impossible, but with God all things are possible.[35]

A triumphant believer operates in the dimension of the supernatural. If one really knows that all things are possible to those who believe,[36] there is nothing to worry about.

157

Fear is not of God. Fear is based upon feelings and appearances, but faith is based upon God's word. Operating in fear is bondage; believers walk in freedom.

> For God hath not given us the spirit of fear; but of power, and of love, and of a sound mind.[37]

When Peter looked at the storm, he sank; as long as he looked to Jesus, he walked on the water.[38] This dramatic instance in Peter's life shows three secrets to victorious Christian living.

Establish God's will. Peter asked Jesus first whether it was His will to let him walk on the water. Before you do anything, find out God's will. Many Christians are walking in foolishness (in the name of living by faith and walking by faith) because of ignorance of God's will. The Body of Christ is hurting because of people who are doing their own thing.

Do His will immediately. When Peter discovered God's will, he did it. He did not wait, seeking counsel from flesh and blood; he obeyed immediately. He left the theologians in the boat to debate whether or not there was scriptural precedence for Peter to walk on water. They are still debating. To listen to them is to miss the Lord.

Look to Jesus. With his eyes on Jesus, Peter walked on the water. The secret of walking through the storms of life is to look at Jesus constantly.

> Looking unto Jesus the author and finisher of our faith; who for the joy that was set before him endured the cross, despising the shame, and is sat down at the right hand of the throne of God.[39]

Be the Best!

Your identity in Jesus is the key to the super-abundant life. Christians who do not know who they are in Christ live in defeat. The devil wants to keep them ignorant of their new place in majesty. This gives him an advantage. He has free access to their riches in Christ, which they let him come in to steal. Most Christians are like the man on the Jericho Road, beaten down, robbed, and stripped by the devil, and in need of the good Samaritan.

There is power ingrained in our new identity in Jesus. We are a generation of kings and priests unto God. Kings think like kings. They live like kings. They act like kings. Queen Elizabeth II is aware of who she is. If Christians would live in the awareness of who they are in Christ, they would experience the abundant life. The true "you" is the you that God says you are.

The word of God is the only place to discover yourself in Christ. Here is who you are in Him, according to God's word:

- A son of God and heir of the kingdom. (Galatians 4:6, 7.)

- God's beloved. (Ephesians 1:6.)

- The temple of God. (1 Corinthians 6:19.)

- The righteousness of God in Christ. (2 Corinthians 5:21.)

- God's workmanship. (Ephesians 2:10.)

These are just a few scriptures to start you on the most dynamic discovery of who you are in Christ. What defeats the devil is not what you have done, but what Jesus has done for you. It is not who you are, but "whose" you are.

The new elite status you have entitles you to special privileges granted only to believers. Because of what God has done for you in Jesus Christ, you are unconquerable:

- Your sins have been forgiven. (Ephesians 1:7.)

- You have been reconciled to God. (Romans 5:10.)

- You have peace with God. (Romans 5:1.)

- You have fellowship with God. (1 John 1:3.)

- You have access to God. (Romans 5:2.)

- You have the Holy Spirit. (Galatians 4:6.)

- You are complete in Him. (Colossians 2:10.)

- You have eternal life. (1 John 5:11.)

In Christ, you have everything you need to be like Him. He paid for it. He has given it to you. It is a gift, free for the taking. You can't earn it. However, the one thing God can't do for you is to force you to receive. God has left the choice up to you.

Those who choose going all the way with Jesus receive all that Jesus has for them. They are the happiest people on the face of the earth. They live like King's kids. They know that everything in time, space, and matter is moving toward their manifestation as the sons of God.

> Because the creature itself also shall be delivered from the bondage of corruption into the glorious liberty of the children of God. For we know that the whole creation groaneth and travaileth in pain together until now.[40]

Receive the Best!

Soteria is a Greek word for "salvation." It includes all these ideas: deliverance from bondage; restoration; complete recovery of spirit, soul, and body—in essence, being made whole. In the Bible, there are three Greek words closely associated with the salvation experience: *makarios*, *chara*, and *agallaisis*.

Makarios means "blessed." Salvation is a blessed experience. It's also translated "happy." It is a happy occasion. Saved people are happy.

Chara means "joy" or "delight." Joy is a state of being. Jesus gives joy to His own.

> These things have I spoken unto you, that my joy might remain in you, and that your joy might be full.[41]

Chara is the secret of the prosperity of the King's kids. It is joy born out of fellowship with God the Father through our Lord Jesus. Paul describes this kind of heaven-born joy as "joy unspeakable and full of glory."[42]

Agallaisis, another Greek word closely linked with salvation, means "exultation." Out of an encounter with God, festivity breaks forth from the innermost part of your being. Salvation is a joyride to heaven. Celebration flows out of gratitude for the fun of riding with God on high places.

Paul described the inspiration of scriptures as *theopneustos*, meaning "to be borne along, to be carried." The writers of the Bible were carried along by the Holy Spirit.[43] You too can be inspired as you study God's word and you can be carried aloft by the Holy Spirit as the Word of God becomes *rhema*, the living word, the word referred to as "quick, and powerful, and sharper than any twoedged sword, piercing even to the dividing asunder of soul and spirit."[44]

African women carry their babies on their backs everywhere they go. This is a picture of what happens to the believer. As he trusts in the Lord with all his heart and leans not unto his own understanding,[45] he becomes dependent for his every need upon the word of God like the African baby is upon his mother. To be led by the Spirit is to be borne along on the wings of the Holy Spirit to new heights in God, as you daily read the word, meditate on the word, and sing the word.

God leads his kids through situations, not around them. He is bigger than the devil. He is bigger than our biggest problems. He is bigger than sickness. He empowers us to overcome.

But ye shall receive power, after that the Holy Ghost is come upon you, and ye shall be witnesses unto me both in Jerusalem, and in all Judea, and in Samaria, and unto the uttermost part of the earth.[46]

God delights to display his power to his children by leading them through the storm. He is not afraid of the devil. God carried Israel through the desert. He didn't carry them around it. He didn't carry them over or under it. He carried them through. My God carries me through.

In 1975, during the civil war in my beloved home country—then called Rhodesia—He carried three ministers through a road full of land mines. The army warned us against going to visit ten missionary couples trapped on the Mozambique border. But the Lord said, "Go." Capetown pastor John vanZyl and Kevin Creasy and I went in obedience to Him. The Spirit of God carried us through 200 miles of the dangerous kill-zone.

God's divine plan for man to be in power and majesty has been fulfilled in Jesus. Everything the devil stole from man at the Fall is restored in Jesus. All the blessings in this life and in heaven have been put to your account in Jesus.

According as His divine power has given unto us *all things that pertain unto life and godliness*, through the knowledge of him that hath called us to glory and virtue.[47]

The devil can never again steal from you, because you have power over him.

Behold, I give unto you power to tread on serpents
and scorpions, and over all the power of the
enemy: and nothing shall by any means hurt you.[48]

The devil robbed and usurped Adam's authority. God
never gave that unique place to Satan, but to man. In the
man Jesus, what Adam lost has been restored to you.
Now, the devil is subject to you, because Jesus came 2000
years ago to put an end to his works.

He that committeth sin is of the devil; for the devil
sinneth from the beginning. For this purpose the
Son of God was manifested, *that He might destroy
the works of the devil.* [49]

As the devil's works affected the whole man in spirit,
soul, and body, so also did the work of Jesus. He
redeemed the whole man in the whole world, and made
available to "whosoever will" super-abundant life.

The thief cometh not, but for to steal, and to kill,
and to destroy: I am come that they might have
life, and that they might have it more
abundantly.[50]

Jesus restores peace to the broken-hearted, joy to the
soul, life to the spirit, and health to the body. The festival
of celebration is born out of coming back home, where we
belong. Jesus is everything that man lost through sin. He
is all we need in order to become what God wants us to
be.

All of heaven is working to bring man not only to the
former glory that was his in the Garden of Eden, but

beyond it. Jesus is preparing a place for us in heaven itself.

Sons of God do not live aimlessly drifting on the sea of life, hoping one day to get to heavenly shores. Children of the Kingdom have already received a down payment and a foretaste of that which is to come. They live in divine well-being.

> Blessed is the man that walketh not in the counsel of the ungodly, nor standeth in the way of sinners, nor sitteth in the seat of the scornful.
>
> But his delight is in the law of the Lord; and in his law doth he meditate day and night.
>
> And he shall be like a tree planted by the rivers of water, that bringeth forth his fruit in his season; his leaf also shall not wither; and whatsoever he doeth shall prosper.[51]

Scripture References

Introduction

1. John 10:10.

2. Luke 8:10.

Chapter 1

1. Hebrews 12:2.

2. 1 Corinthians 2:9.

3. Ephesians 2:10.

4. Deuteronomy 28:1-10.

5. 2 Corinthians 1:20.

6. Romans 8:37.

7. 1 Corinthians 1:30.

Chapter 2

1. Romans 8:2

2. Isaiah 40:31a

3. Ephesians 1:4.

4. Romans 8:37.

5. Romans 8:29; 2 Corinthians 3:18.

6. Ephesians 2:6.

7. Hosea 3:6.

8. Romans 8:37.

9. Revelation 3:14-21.

10. John 10:10b.

11. Psalm 3:3b.

12. Psalm 16:11.

13. Isaiah 54:17a.

14. Romans 8:31b.

15. Philippians 4:19.

16. 1 Peter 2:9.

17. 1 Thessalonians 5:24.

18. Romans 7:18a.

19. John 15:5b.

20. Ephesians 2:10.

21. 1 John 4:4b.

22. Psalm 78:41b.

23. Mark 9:23b.

24. Jeremiah 1:12b.

Chapter 3

1. John 15:4, 5.

2. Galatians 2:20.

3. Matthew 25:34; Ephesians 1:4.

4. Matthew 6:10.

5. Romans 7:18.

6. Genesis 1:11, 12.

7. Matthew 12:30; Luke 11:23.

8. Revelation 3:16.

9. Philippians 2:13.

10. Romans 8:29.

11. Romans 4:17b.

12. Ephesians 2:10.

13. Ezekiel 36:26.

14. Philippians 4:13.

15. Romans 8:33b, 34a.

16. Romans 3:24.

17. Romans 5:1, 2.

18. Romans 7:18, 19.

19. Romans 5:19.

20. Galatians 2:16.

Chapter 4

1. Exodus 12.

2. 2 Corinthians 5:17.

3. 2 Corinthians 5:18; Ephesians 2:16;
Colossians 1:20.

4. Galatians 3:13.

5. Jeremiah 31:33.

6. Hebrews 10:16-22.

7. Hebrews 7:26-8:1.

8. Matthew 26:28.

9. Ephesians 1:13, 14.

10. Hebrews 13:5b.

11. Matthew 4:1-11.

12. 1 John 4:4b.

13. 1 Corinthians 1:30.

14. Romans 8:29; 2 Peter 1:4; 1 John 3:2.

15. John 8:32b.

16. John 16:33b.

17. James 1:6.

18. James 1:22; Matthew 7:26.

19. Proverbs 23:7a.

20. Hebrews 10:23.

21. John 1:14.

22. James 2:26.

Chapter 5

1. Hebrews 11:1.

2. Revelation 22:13.

3. Mark 9:23b.

4. Romans 8:37.

5. James 4:7b.

6. Romans 8:7.

7. Jeremiah 1:21; Romans 4:21.

8. Hebrews 11:3.

9. James 5:16.

10. James 1:6, 7.

11. 1 John 5:14, 15.

12. 1 Kings 8:56.

13. Numbers 23:19.

14. Jeremiah 1:12b.

15. Ephesians 3:20.

16. Jeremiah 29:11.

17. John 10:10.

18. Revelation 22:13.

19. Revelation 4:11.

20. Isaiah 40:15.

21. Revelation 17:14.

22. Romans 4:17b.

23. Galatians 6:8.

24. Luke 22:42b.

25. 1 John 5:14b, 15.

26. 1 Peter 5:8.

27. 1 Corinthians 5:7.

28. Romans 6:11.

29. Philippians 4:13.

30. Ecclesiastes 1:9.

31. Romans 8:26, 27.

32. John 15:26.

33. Romans 8:27.

34. John 16:7.

35. John 15:4.

36. Exodus 19:4.

37. Isaiah 55:9.

38. John 14:6.

39. Romans 1:17.

40. Isaiah 30:21.

41. John 14:26.

Chapter 6

1. 2 Peter 1:4.

2. Ephesians 1:12.

3. Joshua 1:3.

4. Ephesians 2:5, 6.

5. Ephesians 2:10.

6. 2 Corinthians 10:4.

7. John 15:5.

8. 2 Corinthians 3:18.

9. Romans 8:29, 30.

10. Hebrews 13:6.

11. Romans 8:28.

12. Romans 8:37.

13. 2 Timothy 1:12.

14. Hebrews 12:2.

15. Isaiah 54:17.

16. 2 Corinthians 5:20.

17. Romans 8:11.

18. Colossians 1:27.

19. 2 Corinthians 3:5.

20. Philippians 4:13.

21. James 4:10.

22. 1 Peter 3:22.

23. 2 Corinthians 2:14.

24. 1 John 1:7.

25. Hebrews 4:12.

26. 2 Corinthians 10:4.

27. 1 John 1:7.

28. Hebrews 4:12.

29. 2 Peter 1:4.

30. 2 Corinthians 3:18.

Chapter 7

1. 1 Corinthians 2:7.

2. Matthew 25:34; John 1724: Ephesians 1:4.

3. Psalm 3:3.

4. Romans 8:15.

5. John 4:23a.

6. Philippians 3:3.

7. Ephesians 1:6.

8. John 1:14.

9. Hebrews 1:3.

10. 2 Corinthians 4:7.

11. 1 John 3:2.

12. Ruth 4: Galatians 4:5.

13. Romans 8:31-39.

14. 2 Timothy 3:5a.

15. 2 Corinthians 3:6-8.

16. 2 Corinthians 4:10-11.

17. Psalm 78:41.

18. Ephesians 4:30.

19. 1 Kings 18:21.

20. James 1:8.

21. Romans 12:2.

22. Ephesians 6:14.

23. Colossians 1:13.

Chapter 8

1. Genesis 5:24.

2. Acts 17:28.

3. Matthew 17:1-9.

4. Psalm 23:6.

5. Colossians 1:13.

6. Hebrews 13:5.

7. Matthew 28:20.

8. Romans 6:6.

9. Ephesians 4:22-24; Colossians 3:9,10.

10. Proverbs 23:7a.

11. Romans 12, 1, 2.

12. Exodus 34:28-35.

13. Ephesians 2:6.

14. Colossians 1:27.

15. Galatians 2:20.

16. Matthew 7:20.

17. Jeremiah 31:34.

18. Jeremiah 31:34.

19. Ezekiel 36:25.

20. Ezekiel 36:26.

21. Ezekiel 36:27.

22. Ezekiel 36:27.

23. Hebrews 13:5.

24. Hebrews 13:5.

25. Psalm 138:8.

Chapter 9

1. 1 Peter 1:16b.

2. Hebrews 12:14b.

3. Isaiah 64.6.

4. 1 Thessalonians 4:3.

5. John 8:32.

6. Romans 1:16.

7. Matthew 4:4.

8. James 1:22.

9. Matthew 7:21, 24.

10. 1 John 3:8b.

11. 1 Peter 1:8.

12. 1 Peter 5:8.

13. James 1:17.

14. Isaiah 61:3.

15. John 16:7.

16. Romans 8:28.

17. John 15:11.

18. Romans 8:31b.

19. Galatians 4:9.

20. 1 John 4:8.

21. Ephesians 3:19.

Chapter 10

1. 1 Peter 1:8.

2. Galatians 2:20.

3. Philippians 1:21a.

4. John 8:32b.

5. 2 Corinthians 5:21.

6. Romans 8:2.

7. Philippians 2:13.

8. 2 Corinthians 2:14.

9. 2 Chronicles 20:15b.

10. Galatians 4:9.

11. Philippians 1:21.

12. Matthew 4:4.

13. Jeremiah 1:12b.

14. Matthew 24:25.

15. John 10:10.

16. Romans 10:6-8.

17. Psalm 119:11.

18. Galatians 5:22.

19. 2 Timothy 3:5.

20. 2 Corinthians 3:6.

21. Jeremiah 23:6.

22. Ephesians 2:10.

23. Romans 1:17.

24. Hebrews 12:2.

25. Romans 9:23.

26. 1 Peter 1:16.

27. Matthew 6:10.

28. 1 John 5:20.

29. John 14:10.

30. Psalm 23:6b.

31. Acts 13:22.

32. Luke 15:11-32.

33. Philippians 4:7.

Chapter 11

1. Romans 11:29.

2. Ephesians 1:11.

3. Ephesians 2:6.

4. 2 Peter 1:3, 4.

5. Philippians 4:19.

6. Matthew 6:8b.

7. 1 John 5:14b.

8. Psalm 139:13-16.

9. Jeremiah 29:11.

10. John 10:10.

11. Hebrews 12:2.

Chapter 12

1. Matthew 6:10.

2. Ephesians 2:10.

3. Matthew 16:18b.

4. Psalm 37:23.

5. Luke 18:22.

6. Zechariah 4:6.

7. Hebrews 13:21.

8. John 4:34; 14:10.

9. Galatians 4:9.

10. Philippians 4:19.

11. Romans 8:37.

12. Philippians 4:13.

13. Hebrews 13:5.

14. Mark 9:23.

15. 2 Corinthians 5:7.

16. Galatians 3:13.

17. Philippians 4:19.

18. Galatians 2:20.

19. 1 Corinthians 2:9.

20. Ephesians 1:7, 8.

21. Ephesians 4:12, 13.

Chapter 13

1. James 1:2, 3.

2. Hebrews 5:8.

3. Matthew 5:10-12.

4. 2 Corinthians 2:14.

5. John 14:30.

6. Isaiah 55:8, 9.

7. John 4:34.

8. 2 Corinthians 12:9.

9. Romans 8:28.

10. James 1:2-4.

11. Luke 24:49.

12. Philippians 2:13.

13. Hebrews 13:20, 21.

14. Jude 24, 25.

15. 2 Peter 2:9a.

16. 2 Chronicles 20:15.

17. 1 Corinthians 1:8; 1 Thessalonians 5:23;
    2 Timothy 1:12.

18. Romans 8:37.

19. 1 Timothy 2:12; Revelation 5:10.

20. Matthew 28:18-20.

21. Matthew 16:18.

22. Romans 5:14-17.

23. Matthew 12:29.

24. Colossians 2:15.

25. Hebrews 2:14.

26. James 4:7b.

27. Luke 19:13.

28. Proverbs 29:18a.

29. Genesis 12:1-3.

30. Genesis 15:1.

31. Hebrews 11:10.

32. Genesis 13:2.

33. 3 John 2.

34. Psalm 1:1-3.

35. Joshua 1:8.

36. Matthew 6:33.

37. Luke 12:32.

38. Ephesians 2:6.

39. Mark 10:30.

40. John 10:10.

41. 2 Corinthians 4:7.

42. Deuteronomy 28:1-13.

43. Philippians 4:12, 13.

44. Philippians 4:19.

45. 2 Corinthians 8:9.

46. 2 Corinthians 9:8.

47. 1 Peter 1:8.

48. Genesis 37.

49. Galatians 3:13.

50. Romans 8:1.

51. Ephesians 1:3.

52. 1 Corinthians 6:14; Colossians 2:12.

Chapter 14

1. Jeremiah 31:3b.

2. Colossians 2:10.

3. Philippians 4:13.

4. Romans 8:37.

5. 2 Corinthians 3:5, 9:8.

6. Colossians 3:3.

7. 1 John 2:27, 28.

8. Hebrews 1:3a.

9. 2 Corinthians 3:18b.

10. John 17:22.

11. John 15:13.

12. Romans 8:17.

13. Ephesians 1:6b.

14. 1 John 4:18.

15. Galatians 4:9.

16. Romans 8:14,15.

17. Ephesians 3:18, 19.

18. Philippians 3:13, 14.

19. James 1:17.

20. Psalm 84:11.

21. 1 Peter 1:8.

22. Luke 15:11-32.

23. Galatians 4:5.

24. Psalm 23:5, 6.

25. Romans 5:5.

26. John 17:23.

27. Exodus 3:4.

28. Haggai 2:9.

29. Romans 8:37-39.

Chapter 15

1. John 15:8-12.

2. John 17:22.

3. John 13:34, 35.

4. 1 John 3:14-16.

5. 1 John 4:19.

6. 1 Corinthians 2:12.

7. 1 John 4:7-12.

8. Ephesians 5:27.

9. Ephesians 4:16.

10. 2 Corinthians 5:16.

11. Matthew 16:18.

12. 1 Peter 2:5.

13. Romans 8:17.

14. John 14:16, 26; 15:26; 16:7.

15. 2 Corinthians 1:3, 4.

16. Ephesians 3:8.

17. Isaiah 54:2.

18. 2 Corinthians 4:7.

19. 2 Timothy 2:21.

20. 1 John 4:18.

21. 2 Corinthians 3:18.

22. Jeremiah 29:11.

23. Zechariah 4:6.

24. 2 Corinthians 4:7.

25. 2 Corinthians 12:9.

26. Romans 8:37.

27. Genesis 32:22-30.

28. Psalm 3:3.

29. Malachi 4:2.

30. Genesis 49:9-11; Revelation 5:5.

31. Philippians 2:13.

32. Nehemiah 8:10b.

33. Hosea 4:6.

Chapter 16

1. Galatians 3:1.

2. John 15:16.

3. John 17:6.

4. 1 John 4:15; 5:1.

5. John 1:12.

6. Romans 8:14; 1 John 3:1.

7. Romans 4:7.

8. Hebrews 8:10; 10:16.

9. John 15:16.

10. Hebrews 12:2.

11. John 6:28.

12. John 6:29.

13. Mark 9:23.

14. Hebrews 11:6.

15. Genesis 17:1, 2; 28:3; 35:11, 12.

16. 1 John 5:4.

17. 2 Thessalonians 3:3; 2 Timothy 1:12;
Jude 24.

18. John 6:29.

19. Psalm 100:2.

20. Ephesians 3:20.

21. John 15:3.

22. John 8:32b.

23. Romans 1:16.

24. John 17:12b.

25. 1 Corinthians 1:30.

26. Romans 8:7.

27. Isaiah 64:6b.

28. 1 John 5:4, 5.

29. John 15:5b.

30. 1 Peter 5:8.

31. Colossians 1:27.

32. 1 John 4:4b.

33. Galatians 2:20a.

34. John 6:63b.

35. 1 Corinthians 6:19, 20.

36. 1 Corinthians 3:16a.

37. Romans 7:18.

38. Hebrews 13:5b.

39. Romans 8:39.

40. Galatians 2:20b.

41. Philippians 1:21.

42. 1 John 4:18b.

43. 1 Peter 1:8b.

44. Matthew 1:23.

45. John 14:6b.

46. 1 John 3:8b.

47. Romans 8:3, 4.

48. Matthew 4:4b.

49. 2 Timothy 3:5.

50. Luke 17:21.

51. Romans 14:17.

52. John 17:22.

53. 1 John 3:2.

Chapter 17

1. Matthew 5:17a.

2. Romans 8:1-4.

3. Romans 6:6; Galatians 2:20.

4. Romans 8:2.

5. 1 John 1:9.

6. Romans 8:4.

7. Ephesians 2:12-15.

8. Psalm 51:2, 3.

9. 1 John 1:9.

10. Matthew 5:18.

11. 1 Peter 1:16.

12. Romans 13:14.

13. Romans 8:2.

14. 1 John 1:9.

15. Romans 14:17.

16. Galatians 2:20.

17. James 4:7b.

18. John 8:44.

19. John 10:10.

20. Hebrews 4:3.

21. Isaiah 10:27; Matthew 11:30.

22. Luke 4:18.

23. Isaiah 61:3.

24. Romans 8:39b.

25. Romans 8:31.

26. Ephesians 2:10.

27. Romans 8:1, 4.

28. John 8:32.

29. John 17:17.

30. John 17:17.

31. Luke 17:21.

32. Colossians 1:27.

33. 2 Corinthians 3:6b.

34. Matthew 4:4.

35. 1 John 4:4.

36. 1 Corinthians 1:30; 2 Corinthians 5:21;
Ephesians 2:14.

37. John 15:5-16.

38. Philippians 1:6.

39. Hebrews 10:19-22.

40. Ephesians 1:6.

41. 2 Corinthians 3:18.

42. Hebrews 12:2.

43. Philippians 3:8-14.

Chapter 18

1. John 1:16, 17.

2. Galatians 2:20.

3. Galatians 3:11.

4. Philippians 2:13.

5. John 14:19.

6. 1 Corinthians 6:14.

7. Ephesians 2:15; 4:24; Colossians 3:10.

8. Jude 1:24.

9. Hebrews 13:5.

10. Psalm 23:6; 27:4; 61:4.

11. Colossians 3:3.

12. John 10:28.

13. 2 Corinthians 12:9.

14. Romans 8:35.

15. Ephesians 2:6.

16. Romans 8:17.

17. 2 Peter 1:3.

18. 1 Peter 5:1.

19. John 17: 22, 23.

20. Luke 12:32.

21. Isaiah 61:3.

22. 1 John 3:2.

23. 1 John 4:17.

24. 2 Corinthians 3:18.

25. Colossians 1:27.

26. Ephesians 1:3-6.

27. John 15:26.

28. John 15:5.

29. Galatians 3:1-3.

30. Romans 7:8.

31. 2 Corinthians 2:14.

32. 1 Corinthians 6:19, 20.

33. Ephesians 2:8-10.

Chapter 19

1. Genesis 1:26.

2. Galatians 4:5, 6.

3. John 15:4.

4. Psalm 16:11.

5. Psalm 91:1.

6. Hebrews 12:2.

7. Philippians 3:14.

8. Galatians 3:13.

9. Romans 8:38, 39.

10. Revelation 5:11, 12.

11. Romans 4:20-22.

12. Hebrews 13:15.

13. Psalm 34:1.

14. Colossians 1:12 (ASV).

15. 2 Corinthians 9:15.

16. Colossians 2:7.

17. 1 Thessalonians 5:18.

18. Luke 18:43.

19. Philippians 4:4.

20. Romans 8:28.

21. Deuteronomy 28:6.

22. 1 John 5:4, 5.

23. 2 Corinthians 5:7.

24. John 16:33.

25. 2 Corinthians 10:4.

26. Matthew 11:28-30.

27. 1 Samuel 2:18.

28. Ephesians 6:14-17.

29. Acts 19:13-17.

30. Ephesians 6:12.

31. 2 Corinthians 10:4.

32. Deuteronomy 20:4.

33. Hebrews 4:9, 10.

34. 2 Corinthians 2:14.

35. Matthew 19:26.

36. Mark 9:23.

37. 2 Timothy 1:7.

38. Matthew 14:24-32.

39. Hebrews 12:2.

40. Romans 8:21, 22.

41. John 15:11.

42. 1 Peter 1:8.

43. 2 Timothy 3:16.

44. Hebrews 4:12.

45. Proverbs 3:5.

46. Acts 1:8.

47. 2 Peter 1:3.

48. Luke 10:19.

49. 1 John 3:8.

50. John 10:10.

51. Psalm 1:1-3.

About the Author

Robert Mawire, Founder and President of Hope for Africa and Good News World Outreach, an evangelistic and missionary organization reaching out to the lost world, has ministered the gospel for over 20 years. He is a sought after conference speaker. He is a host of a global broadcasting program, the Hour of Good News, heard on six continents of the world. He has been featured on the 700 Club, NBC, 20/20, American Journal, and numerous newspapers and magazines.

Robert lives in Fort Worth, Texas, with his Australian wife, Janet, and their three sons, Jonathan, Caleb, and Stephen. Their global ministry is based in Fort Worth.

Order Form

Good News World
P. O. Box 895, Fort Worth, TX 76101
E-mail: hope@goodnewsworld.org

Top Secrets Revealed

Cost: _____ Copies x **$10.00**   _____

Shipping and Handling $ 2.50

Total   _____

Payment: Check ____   Money Order ____   MasterCard/Visa ____

Card Number: _____

Name on Card: _____

Ship to:

_____

_____

_____

_____